Psychology and Education

Psychology and Education provides a user-friendly introduction to educational psychology. The book covers psychological theories and their practical applications in education. Susan Bentham has written an ideal guide to this topic for students studying the OCR A level specification. The book will also be relevant to those studying the Edexcel specification and to those with a general interest in education and learning.

The book covers the cognitive, behaviourist and humanistic perspectives on learning, including the works of Piaget, Vygotsky, Bruner and others, and describes the practical application of these theories. The assessment of educational performance is covered and the cultural and developmental factors affecting performance are discussed. Chapters on the special educational needs of the educationally disadvantaged and gifted, and on disruptive behaviour in school are included, with sections on ADHD, autism and dyslexia. The book also discusses teaching and learning styles, and the design and layout of educational environments.

The book requires little or no background knowledge and makes an ideal introduction for students of psychology, trainee teachers, child carers and anyone who is interested in what is happening in today's schools.

Susan Bentham is an experienced Psychology A level teacher and examiner for the AQA examination board.

Routledge Modular Psychology

Series editors: Cara Flanagan is a Reviser for AS and A2 level Psychology and lectures at Inverness College. Philip Banyard is Associate Senior Lecturer in Psychology at Nottingham Trent University and a Chief Examiner for AS and A2 level Psychology. Both are experienced writers.

The *Routledge Modular Psychology* series is a completely new approach to introductory-level psychology, tailor-made to the new modular style of teaching. Each short book covers a topic in more detail than any large textbook can, allowing teacher and student to select material exactly to suit any particular course or project.

The books have been written especially for those students new to higher-level study, whether at school, college or university. They include specially designed features to help with technique, such as a model essay at an average level with an examiner's comments to show how extra marks can be gained. The authors are all examiners and teachers at the introductory level.

The *Routledge Modular Psychology* texts are all user-friendly and accessible and include the following features:

- practice essays with specialist commentary to show how to achieve a higher grade
- chapter summaries to assist with revision
- progress and review exercises
- glossary of key terms
- summaries of key research
- further reading to stimulate ongoing study and research
- cross-referencing to other books in the series

Also available in this series (titles listed by syllabus section):

ATYPICAL DEVELOPMENT AND ABNORMAL BEHAVIOUR

Psychopathology
John D. Stirling and Jonathan S.E. Hellewell

Therapeutic Approaches in Psychology
Susan Cave

Classification and Diagnosis of Abnormal Psychology
Susan Cave

BIO-PSYCHOLOGY

Cortical Functions
John Stirling

The Physiological Basis of Behaviour: Neural and hormonal processes
Kevin Silber

Awareness: Biorhythms, sleep and dreaming
Evie Bentley

COGNITIVE PSYCHOLOGY

Memory and Forgetting
John Henderson

Perception: Theory, development and organisation
Paul Rookes and Jane Willson

Attention and Pattern Recognition
Nick Lund

DEVELOPMENTAL PSYCHOLOGY

Early Socialisation: Sociability and attachment
Cara Flanagan

Social and Personality Development
Tina Abbott

PERSPECTIVES AND RESEARCH

Controversies in Psychology
Philip Banyard

Ethical Issues and Guidelines in Psychology
Cara Flanagan and Philip Banyard (forthcoming)

Introducing Research and Data in Psychology: A guide to methods and analysis
Ann Searle

Theoretical Approaches in Psychology
Matt Jarvis

Debates in Psychology
Andy Bell (forthcoming)

SOCIAL PSYCHOLOGY

Social Influences
Kevin Wren

Interpersonal Relationships
Diana Dwyer

Social Cognition
Donald C. Pennington

COMPARATIVE PSYCHOLOGY

The Determinants of Animal Behaviour
JoAnne Cartwright (forthcoming)

Evolutionary Explanations of Human Behaviour
John Cartwright

Animal Cognition
Nick Lund (forthcoming)

OTHER TITLES

Sport Psychology
Matt Jarvis

Health Psychology
Anthony Curtis

Psychology and Work
Christine Hodson

Psychology and Crime
David Putwain and Aidan Sammons (forthcoming)

STUDY GUIDE

Exam Success in AQA(A) Psychology
Paul Humphreys (forthcoming)

To the memory of my mother, Patricia Byrne,
a very special lady!

Psychology and
Education

Susan Bentham

MT

First published 2002
by Routledge
27 Church Road, Hove,
East Sussex, BN3 2FA

Simultaneously published in the USA and Canada
by Routledge
29 West 35th Street, New York, NY 10001

Routledge is an imprint of the Taylor and Francis Group

© 2002 Susan Bentham

Typeset in Times and Frutiger by Keystroke,
Jacaranda Lodge, Wolverhampton
Printed and bound in Great Britain
by TJ International, Padstow, Cornwall

Cover design by Terry Foley

British Library Cataloguing in Publication Data
A catalogue record for this book is available from the British Library

Library of Congress Cataloging-in-Publication Data
A catalog record for this book has been requested

ISBN 0–415–22762–3 (hbk)
ISBN 0–415–22763–1 (pbk)

3/3/03

Contents

Illustrations

Figures

Tables

Acknowledgements

Susan Bentham would like to thank Phil, Cara and Rachel for their helpful comments and support. The author would also like to thank her family for their patience, her students, from whom she has learnt a lot, and her friends.

The author and the publishers would like to thank Constable Publishers and all the copyright holders for material reproduced in this book who have kindly granted permission for their work to be included. Every effort was made to contact authors and copyright holders but, in the event that proper acknowledgement has not been made, the copyright holder should contact the publisher.

Perspectives on learning: the cognitive approach

Introduction

This chapter describes the study of how thinking, or what psychologists term **cognition**, develops and changes over time. Therefore, theories of cognitive development deal with how we learn to think and reason. In this chapter we will be looking both at how we learn and specifically at concepts such as stages of development and maturational readiness. This might seem like a dry academic pursuit carried out by wizened professors in dusty libraries, but it has enormous consequences in the real world, particularly in the field of teaching. How theorists explain the process of learning in part determines teaching methods.

Piaget

Jean Piaget (1896–1980) was a Swiss scholar who began to study children's intellectual development at the beginning of the twentieth century. Early in his career Piaget worked for Albert Binet who was involved in the development of early IQ tests. Piaget's job was to give children questions and to score their answers as correct or not. What intrigued Piaget was not so much whether the children could answer the questions correctly but the fact that children of similar ages were making similar mistakes and that children's thinking was qualitatively different from adult thinking. In other words, the way a child made sense of and interpreted the world was very different from that of an adult. This will come as no surprise to anyone who has spent any time with an inquisitive 4-year-old. From this insight Piaget went on to develop a comprehensive theory of intellectual development.

Piaget's theory is a stage theory. The stages of cognitive development according to Piaget are:

- **Sensori-motor stage** (birth to age 2)
- **Pre-operational stage** (ages 2–7)
- **Concrete operational stage** (ages 7–11)
- **Formal operational stage** (ages 11–12+)

Piaget stated that these stages formed an invariant sequence, meaning that all individuals, everywhere, go through these stages in the same order. The age ranges mentioned by Piaget were set as guidelines; some children would advance earlier or later to the next stage. The key point is that each stage involves a qualitatively different and progressively more complex way of thinking. Successive stages or more complex ways of thinking build upon previous stages or less complex ways of thinking. Piaget stated that at no point could an individual miss or skip a stage.

Piaget's theory stresses the interaction between an individual's level of maturation and an environment that offers the right experiences. According to Piaget, a child actively constructs their knowledge of the world and in that sense is seen as a little scientist. Piaget sees the ultimate goal of mature thinking as the realisation of logic and abstract thinking (Wood 1998). Piaget's theory is comprehensive in that Piaget aimed to explain intellectual growth from birth until adulthood. He looked at intellectual development in a number of areas including: an understanding of physical quantities (i.e. volume, mass, area); number; language; play; and moral development. In order to explain his ideas Piaget created his own distinctive terminology.

Key concepts

Schemas according to Piaget are organised patterns or units of action or thought that we construct to make sense of our interactions with the world. Schemas can be likened to files in which we store information. Piaget believed that thought is internalised action (Piaget 1971). An individual interacts with and explores the environment around them, and it is this physical interaction that becomes internalised to create thought.

Adaptation is a term Piaget used to describe changes an individual makes in response to the environment. Adaptation comprises **assimilation** and **accommodation**. Assimilation, put simply, is taking in new information and trying to fit this information into existing schemas, or responding to the environment in terms of previously learned patterns of behaviour or schemas. Accommodation is changing/modifying existing schemas to fit the new information, or responding to the environment in a new manner, as previously learned patterns of behaviour or schemas are not sufficient. When the individual's perception of the world fits into existing schemas then there is equilibrium or balance. When existing schemas cannot deal with new experiences there is dis-equilibrium. Piaget believed that dis-equilibrium would be experienced as unpleasant, and that individuals being driven by a need to make sense of their world would consequently strive for cognitive balance through the creation of new schemas. For example, let us suppose that an individual has decided to take up sailing. They have never been on a boat before but the idea has always appealed to them, so they sign up for lessons. The first lesson arrives and nothing they have ever done in the past has prepared them for learning this new skill. In Piagetian terms they have no existing schemas for sailing, and this creates an unpleasant feeling of being totally overwhelmed by all the new information. Piaget would call this unpleasant state dis-equilibrium and he would say that this would motivate the individual to create new schemas relating to how to sail.

In the following example fill in the blanks using the following phrases:

new experiences   cognitive equilibrium   accommodate   assimilation
dis-equilibrium   existing schemas

A 2-year-old child is at the zoo with her mother looking at the ducks.

Child: 'Duck'
Mother: 'Yes. That's right. What a nice duck!'

(*Here the child's perception of the world is in agreement with* _____

_____. *The child is in a state of*_____.

This is an example of _____.)

Mother and child move on to the next cage.

Child: 'That's a dinosaur.'
Mother: 'No! That's actually a rhinoceros.'

(*Here the child's existing schemas do not fit the* _____. *The
child is in a state of*_____ *and will be motivated to*

_____.)

Child: 'Rhii-no-saw-rus'
Mother: 'That's right.'

(*Piaget assumes that the discrepancy between the child's perception of the
world as reflected in his or her existing schemas and new experiences will be
motivation enough for the development of new schemas. But could the child
not equally react as follows*)

Child: 'No Dinosaur! Dinosaur! Dinosaur! Me like dinosaurs! That's a
dinosaur!'

How would Piaget account for this?

(Answers on p. 181)

Sensori-motor stage (0–2)

This stage sees the emergence of schemas, the development of **object permanence** and **general symbolic function**.

Object permanence is the ability to realise that objects/people exist in space and time even if we cannot see them. Put simply: 'does a coat still exist if we hang it up in the closet and close the door?'

General symbolic function includes the beginning of language, make-believe play and deferred imitation. Deferred imitation is the ability to imitate in the absence of the object or event. Imagine the following situation: a small child at a mothers and toddlers' morning watches another child have a tantrum. The small child's mother proclaims smugly that her son doesn't throw tantrums. Two days later she is preparing her son's tea when he asks for a biscuit. The mother says no and to her dismay her son throws a tantrum. He kicks. He bites. He screams. Her son has mastered what Piaget would call deferred imitation.

Pre-operational stage (2–7)

One of the key achievements of the sensori-motor stage was the emergence of general symbolic function, and it is this ability to use language, to imitate and to engage in pretend play that really takes off and expands during the pre-operational years. However, for all the accomplishments of children within these years, Piaget noted limitations in regard to logical thinking. Limitations include the inability to **decentre** and **conserve** and faulty views in regard to **egocentrism**.

Egocentrism

Piaget defined this not as being selfish but as being unable to take another's point of view or simply believing that everyone sees the world as you do. When a child can see the world from another person's point of view, the child is said to have the ability to decentre. To decentre involves the cognitive ability to hold and understand two apparently opposing views.

To test for egocentrism, children were presented with a three-dimensional model of three mountains: one with snow on it, one with a cabin on it and the last with a cross on top. The child sat at the table looking at the model and a doll was placed at another vantage-point on the other side of the table. The child was shown a selection of pictures representing the mountains. The child was first asked to select the picture that best represented what he/she saw and then to select the picture that best represented what the doll saw. Piaget found that it was not until the child was 9 that he/she could accurately select the picture that corresponded to what the doll saw.

Evaluation of egocentrism

To evaluate egocentrism, one can evaluate both the research regarding egocentrism and the nature of the concept, that is, what does egocentrism really mean? In regard to the research, Hughes (1975) aimed to replicate Piaget's study on egocentrism but with the important difference that he wanted to create a test that made more sense to the average child. Hughes made a model, which consisted of four walls set up in a criss-cross shape. Hughes used two boy dolls and a policeman doll in what was essentially a game of hide and seek. The child would be standing over the model. The policeman doll would be placed at the end of a wall where it could see into two sections, and the child would be asked to place the boy doll where the policeman couldn't see it. The point of the study is that there would be a conflict between what the child could see from his/her viewpoint and what the doll could see from its viewpoint. While according to Piaget children do not have the ability to take another's point of view until they are 9 years old, Hughes found otherwise. When the task was such that it made sense to the child, the child had no problem in responding. Hughes found that 90 per cent of children, aged three and a half to five, were successful in this task.

Egocentrism can also be evaluated by questioning what is meant by the concept of taking another's viewpoint. Do the following examples illustrate the concept of egocentrism as Piaget defined it?

- If a child is given £5 to buy mummy a present, at what age would the child realise that what mummy wants for her birthday will not be the same as what the child would like?
- When do children learn to tell white lies in order to save someone's feelings? 'Yes Grandma, I really like those striped socks that you knitted for me.'

There are no definite answers to these questions; the point being that egocentrism is difficult to define.

Conservation involves the realisation that an object remains the same even though its appearance changes. Conservation can apply to concepts such as substance, length, number, liquid and area. In the standard test for conservation of number a child sees two identical rows of beads. The experimenter asks the child if the two rows are the same. The experimenter then makes one row appear to be longer by increasing the space between the beads. The child is then asked which line has more beads.

1 O O O O   2   O O O O

   O O O O   O O O O

Young children will typically state that the longest-looking line has the most. For young children appearance is all. It is not until the age of 6 or 7 that children will realise that each row despite its appearance still contains the same number of beads. Piaget believed that children failed to conserve as they were unable to simultaneously hold in their minds the properties of the material, that is the number of beads, and the appearance of the properties – that is, how the beads are spaced out. Similarly children at this age fail to conserve as they are unable to mentally reverse an action: that is, to realise that what has been done can be undone.

In order to appreciate the complexities involved in conservation tasks it is helpful to consider the following issues.

- How do we phrase the question? Taking the example of conservation of number, do we say: 'Do they have the same number?' 'Do they have the same amount?' 'Are they the same?'
- Does the manner in which the question is phrased affect the child's response?

- How can we be sure that we are not leading or suggesting an answer to the child?
- How can we ascertain whether children do in fact understand the question?
- How many times should we ask the question? Rose and Blank (1974) stated that one reason for failure to conserve might be the fact that, in a standard Piagetian conservation experiment, the experimenter asks the child the question 'are they the same?' twice, once before the change and once afterwards. In attempting to make sense of what the adult is doing, a child might assume that, since the adult asked the same question a second time, perhaps a different answer is expected.
- How does the child interpret the changes? Perhaps the child compares what the experimenter is doing to a magic trick. McGarrigle and Donaldson (1974) carried out a revised version of the conservation of number test with a Naughty Teddy doll. In this experiment it was Naughty Teddy who made the line of beads appear longer. In this revised version more children between the ages of 4 and 6 conserved. In this study the children had a ready explanation for why the appearance of the rows changes. Naughty Teddy had messed the line up. This test made more sense to the average child.

However, in support of Piaget's views, older children do solve these conservation problems with greater ease, reflecting a qualitative change in thinking.

Concrete operational stage (7 –11) and formal operational stage (11+)

Piaget stated that for every weakness in the pre-operational stage there is strength in the concrete operational stage. Children have acquired **mental operations**. They have acquired logical rules regarding addition, subtraction and reversibility. Children will pass the tests of conservation. Conservation of substance, length, number and liquid is achieved for most children by 6 or 7, with conservation of area not being achieved until age 9 or 10. However, Piaget felt that there was still more to acquire in that operations could only be carried out if the objects were actually present or imaginable, hence the stage of concrete operations. Children at this stage would not be able to think in terms of abstractions; this ability, the culmination of the development of logic, would be achieved during the formal operational stage.

Evaluation of Piagetian theory

There are several criticisms that can be made of Piaget's theory.

1 Do all individuals of 11 or 12 really think as Piaget envisioned? The answer is basically no. It has been said that just as Piaget under-estimated the abilities of young children he overestimated the ability of older individuals. Keating (1980) estimates that only about 50–60 per cent of 18- or 20-year-olds seem to use formal operations at all and of those not all of them use this pattern of thought consistently. Other theorists state that perhaps some adults are never capable of formal operational thinking (Papalia 1972; Rubin *et al.* 1973).

2 Piaget also stated that all individuals go through the stages in the same order though the age at which they progress to the next stage will differ. If this is true then we can ask what factors account for individual differences? Piaget did not address these issues (Wood 1998).

3 Piaget assumed that the discrepancy between existing schemas and the child's perception of the world would be motivation for the development of new schemas. However, the question remains as to whether a discrepancy alone would be sufficient motivation.

4 It was stated earlier that Piaget, in order to explain his ideas, created his own distinctive terminology; therefore we need to realise that Piagetian terms such as schema are hypothetical constructs. On one level we could ask where is the proof that schemas exist? No one has ever seen a schema. Brain-scanning techniques have not yet revealed one. However, regardless of proof, hypothetical constructs serve a useful purpose as they attempt to convey an image of how we think.

In summary, Piaget's contribution to developmental psychology has been monumental. Piaget's theory has led to all sorts of applications in the real world. But perhaps the greatest tribute to Piaget's work is the amount of research it has generated. It is this research that has led not only to criticisms of Piaget's original theory but also to a greater understanding of cognitive development.

Vygotsky

Vygotsky (1896–1934) was an eminent Russian psychologist, who was interested in psychology, cultural activity, literature, art and history. Vygotsky's work began to be translated into English in the 1960s and continues to be influential.

Vygotsky saw knowledge as being imparted by experienced adults who would inform or teach the inexperienced. In this way the young child was seen as an apprentice. This is in contrast to Piaget's view where the young child was seen as a little scientist, inventing knowledge for him- or herself, unaided.

Vygotsky believed that we are born with what he referred to as **elementary mental functions**; these are natural unlearned capacities such as attending or sensing. The pre-verbal infant would be governed by these elementary mental functions. Non-human animals, such as apes, would also be governed by elementary mental functions. It is language, which is learned through social interactions, that will ultimately make possible thought, problem solving or what Vygotsky termed **higher mental functions**.

Zone of Proximal Development and scaffolding

It has been said that the **Zone of Proximal Development** (ZPD) is one of Vygotsky's most useful concepts. Vygotsky believed that there was a difference between what an individual could achieve by themselves and what they could do with help from a more skilled individual. This view places an importance on the role of instruction in that what an individual can do today with help he can do tomorrow by himself.

In a sense the ZPD refers to an individual's potential to learn. In fact Vygotsky defined intelligence as the potential to learn. This view takes into account individual differences. Two children may be at the same ability level in a certain subject area at a certain point in time but differ in their ability to learn. To further complicate issues, children could have a different Zone of Proximal Development for different subject areas. For example, Bill and John both started to learn to drive at the same time. Bill took fifteen lessons and passed his driving test whilst John is currently on his fortieth lesson and still doesn't have a hope of passing. However, John learned how to skateboard more quickly than Bill.

Scaffolding is a process whereby, through the language of a shared communication, a more skilled individual is trying to impart knowledge to a less skilled individual. Scaffolding describes the various types of support given by teachers to support the learning of students. Scaffolding is more than a skilled individual instructing a less skilled individual. In Vygotskian terms that would just involve the student being controlled or regulated by the language of the other. To learn, the individual must internalise the instructions of the other in order to self-regulate. Wertsch (1984) stated that for the transformation between other- and self-regulation to take place there must be **intersubjectivity** and **semiotic mediation**.

Jamieson (1994) gives the analogy of a mother trying to teach her child to do a certain task. To begin with, the child's understanding of the task may be so different from the mother's understanding that in a sense they are looking at two different problems. A common understanding of the situation must be negotiated so that both individuals have a shared understanding of what the task entails and what they are supposed to do. This shared understanding is termed intersubjectivity, and the process whereby they achieve this shared understanding is called semiotic mediation. For example, in coming to a shared understanding of new concepts, such as those Vygotsky talks about, we are trying to achieve intersubjectivity. We achieve this shared understanding, intersubjectivity, by both reading information on Vygotsky and discussing these issues with each other. It is for this reason that Vygotsky sees the role of language as crucial to cognitive development.

Bruner

Bruner, an American psychologist, came to study the cognitive development of children after first looking at problem-solving abilities. It has been said that Bruner stands somewhere between Piaget and Vygotsky in terms of his views. Bruner, like Piaget, would acknowledge the role of biology in cognitive development, in particular that individuals are born with biological systems that enable them to make sense of their environment and that these systems mature or become increasingly more complex over time. Bruner would also agree with Piaget that individuals have to be active in their development, that they need to construct their own understanding of the world. However, unlike Piaget and more in agreement with Vygotsky, Bruner emphasises the role of language, that language not only reflects experience but can transform it. Bruner was particularly interested in the language of learning and teaching and expanded on Vygotsky's concept of scaffolding.

Modes of processing information

Bruner outlined three ways or modes of processing information. These are:

- **Enactive representation**: here the baby interacts with its environment in a very physical way. The baby learns to control its body and learns how to act physically upon its environment. This form of memory could be likened to a muscle memory. We learn first how to crawl, then walk and finally run. This knowledge is encoded in our muscles. This type of learning continues throughout our lifetime and is evident when we learn a new skill such as touch-typing, driving or sailing. As the child matures, other modes of processing information become available.
- **Iconic mode**: this mode develops from the age of 1, and here, as the name suggests, incoming information is stored in the form of mental images or pictures (icons). This mode of representation could also take the form of sound or smell images. Bruner explains the failure of children to conserve (recall Piaget's classic studies) as being due to the fact that children are dominated by the iconic mode.
- The **symbolic mode** of representation develops around the age of 7. Again like Piaget, Bruner sees this ability as marking an important shift in cognitive development. The encoding of symbols or rules of thought allows children to pass tests of conservation.

A key difference between Piaget and Bruner is that whilst Piaget thought the application of logic was the ultimate goal of cognitive development, Bruner believed that all these modes of representation were available to and necessary to the adult engaged in problem-solving activities. Bruner believed that different tasks would necessarily need different strategies.

Applications

In this chapter we have discussed how various theorists have attempted to explain how children think and how their thinking develops over time. We will now look at how various theories have been translated into classroom practice.

Maturational readiness

Maturational readiness assumes that at certain ages individuals become cognitively capable of learning certain concepts. Imagine the following example: a mother questions her child's Year 1 teacher about her child's difficulty in reading. The teacher replies that: 'All children are different and all children learn at different rates. Jessica is having difficulty learning to read because she is not quite ready. When she is ready, she will begin to read. It is early days. Just give her time.' In this example the teacher is talking about maturational readiness. According to Piaget, children cannot learn a concept before they are ready. You cannot speed up development. In fact teaching a child a concept before they are ready prevents the child from discovering it for themselves and thus limits their understanding of the concept (Piaget 1970a). However, Bruner and Vygotsky believe that you can speed up or accelerate cognitive development. If language forms thought then we can enhance the cognitive process and increase the quality of our thinking through teaching the appropriate language. Here we need to recall Vygotsky's concept of intersubjectivity, that is, coming to a shared understanding through language or dialogue.

In one study, Wood, Bruner and Ross (1976) attempted to teach 3- and 4-year-old children to assemble a complicated block pyramid. It was felt that it was not until the age of 7 that a child would be in a state of maturational readiness and would be able to do this task without assistance. The children were instructed by their mothers in how to do the task. Some children benefited from instruction while others did not. So can language instruction enhance or accelerate cognitive development? It would seem that the issue is not whether the use of language enhances cognitive skills, but what factors regarding the language of communication are responsible for cognitive development. Wood, Bruner and Ross (1976) found the following:

*Techniques that **did not work**:*

- Strategies that had tutors showing the child what to do first (i.e. 'Now watch what I do. Now you try it') did not work. The authors speculated that this approach overloaded the child's powers of concentration.

- Strategies that relied on verbal instructions (i.e. 'Put the big one there, and the small one there') did not work. Again the authors speculated that children did not understand the commands without the commands being acted out.

*Techniques that **did work***

- Contingent instruction – that is, specific instructions geared to the child's perceived need – seemed to be the most effective. This involved two main rules: when struggling, offer more help; and when succeeding, withdraw help.

Piaget: discovery learning

Piaget wrote volumes regarding cognitive development, but said very little about how his ideas should be translated into the classroom. He left others to make the connections. Piaget would see the learner as active. Thought is internalised action. This would imply that the products of learning need to be produced through an individual acting upon and exploring their environment, hence the concept of **discovery learning**. Motivation to learn, or to create new schemas, would be the result of the individual's awareness of a discrepancy between their existing schemas and the reality of the world. In this sense, motivation is internal. An individual's drive to understand and make sense of the world provides the motivating force behind learning.

Piaget states that children's cognitive development progresses in stages; therefore more simple concepts need to be learned before complex concepts. In terms of what to teach, Piaget stressed the development of logic in several areas including number language and physical quantities.

The role of the teacher in the learning process would be to assess what a child can do and then provide activities or ask questions that create the need to expand existing schemas or to create new schemas. The teacher's aim is to provide opportunities where dis-equilibrium will occur. Interacting with other children could also provide these opportunities. If a child realised that other children had different viewpoints this could provide a source of socio-cognitive conflict that would encourage the development of new schemas.

Of course this view does pose some practical difficulties. Assessing each student in terms of what they know, knowing exactly what to ask them and what activities to give to them to provide dis-equilibrium, could prove challenging to the teacher.

An example of discovery learning

Activity: Birthday Money   *Target group*: Years 3 and 4
Learning objective: Addition and Subtraction

Instructions for playing the game:
Each child starts with a sum of money. Play money is ideal for this game. Children placed in a circle take turns giving the child on their left a birthday present of money. Each child says something like: 'Happy birthday. Here is four pounds.' The child receiving the money has to say how much they have now, e.g. 'I did have £20 and now I have £24.' The child who gave the money has to say how much they have left.

(Atkinson 1999)

Questions

1 Describe the Circle Game in terms of Piaget's view of discovery learning. (The following instructions may help.)

- Get into small groups and try this game. Have one individual act as the teacher and the others as students. The teacher will need to give out play money to all the students in the group. One student will start by giving another student some birthday money, as described above. After everyone in your group has had a turn, discuss whether you think this game is a good example of discovery learning.

- Now repeat this exercise, only now the 'students' are required to have extreme difficulty in doing this task. What questions can the teacher or more able students ask to promote assimilation and accommodation, that is, to promote an understanding of the concepts?

- Are there any problems with this approach?

Progress exercise 1.2

Bruner: discovery learning

Bruner agreed with Piaget that knowledge needed to be constructed, and saw the student as active in the learning process, hence again discovery learning. One of Bruner's key concepts relating to education refers to the **spiral curriculum** (see Table 1.1). The spiral curriculum develops and re-develops concepts at different ages with increasing complexity. Bruner (1963) stated that any aspect of the curriculum can be taught effectively and in some intellectually honest form to any child at any developmental stage. The manner in which the subject is taught should reflect the mode of thinking in which the child is operating. Bruner would argue that as an individual progresses from an enactive to an iconic to a symbolic mode of representation so a teaching programme should progress from a physical experience of the concept, to a concrete visual representation of that concept, to finally a symbolic representation.

In Bruner's view the teacher has a key role in facilitating the development of an individual's coding systems, but other children, particularly a more competent peer, could provide support in the context of scaffolding (Mercer 1995). We will return to the concept of scaffolding, but first let's imagine that we have the task of presenting the concept of fractions to a child at various ages.

Applications of Vygotsky

There are two key concepts outlined by Vygotsky which have particular relevance to teaching; one is the Zone of Proximal Development and the other is the technique of scaffolding. The Zone of Proximal Development is the gap between what an individual can learn by themselves and what an individual can learn with the help of others. Such a view places the emphasis on effective instruction as key to the learning process. The teacher or a more able peer could give effective instruction. Vygotsky (Mercer 1995) states that instruction is only effective when it is slightly ahead of the child's developmental level. Vygotsky's view implies that an individual left to their own devices to construct knowledge for themselves is unlikely to be stretching their intellectual capabilities (Mercer 1995). Vygotsky would further state that instruction needs to be targeted to the individual's Zone of Proximal Development. The question is how can a teacher assess a child's potential or ZPD? How does a teacher know whether the instructions given are under- or overestimating a child's ability? More importantly, what form should this instruction take?

Vygotsky felt that individuals should be taught via a process called scaffolding. The concept of scaffolding has been taken up and expounded by other theorists, notably Bruner. But what is scaffolding?

Table 1.1 The spiral curriculum

Stage	Example of teaching style
Enactive A child under the age of 1 learns by physically acting on its environment. Memory is encoded within the muscles.	A very young child could be given a large chocolate chip biscuit. The child could be encouraged to break the biscuit in half and to share the biscuit.
Iconic A child between the ages of 1 and 7 uses mental images based on sight, hearing, smell or touch.	A class of 5-year-olds is asked to draw several large cakes on pieces of paper. They then get into pairs and are told that they are going to have a tea party and that they will need to share their cakes evenly with the other members. The children will have to cut their cakes into halves. Then the children will be asked to join another group. Now there will be four members to the group and they will need to cut the cakes into quarters.
Symbolic Individuals of 7 and above are able to represent ideas through symbols or rules.	A class of 8-year-olds is divided into groups of four. Each child is asked to write a fraction on a large card, but to do so in secret. The children are then asked to show each other their fractions and to put them in order.

Example of scaffolding

Let's suppose a teacher is trying to help a 10-year-old with multiplication. The conversation could go something like this:

Scott: 'Miss, I can't do this!'
Teacher: 'OK Scott, now what is this question asking?'
Scott: 'Twelve times fourteen.'
Teacher: 'That's right Scott, do you remember what we do first?'
Scott: 'No. I don't know.'
Teacher: 'Have a go.'
Scott: 'You do four times two, that's eight and then you do four times one, that's four.'
Teacher: 'Ok, write that down, that's good. Now what next?'
Scott: 'You times one times two, that's two, and then you do one times one and that's one and then you write it down. I don't know where to write it'
Teacher: 'You are remembering that this is the tricky bit. Now one is in the tens column and you need to do what?'
Scott: 'That's right, I need to line the answer under the tens column. Now I add the numbers together and the answer is 168.'
Teacher: 'Well done Scott!'

(Adapted from Mercer 1995)

As the above example shows, there is quite an art to scaffolding. It would have been easier for the teacher to say go and try to do this by yourself, or to say just watch what I do, or to just tell Scott what the answer was. But that wouldn't be scaffolding. Scaffolding incorporates the principles of contingent instructions, that is, offer more help when the student is struggling and withdraw help when the student is succeeding.

Summary

This chapter has looked at three theorists within the cognitive approach to learning. Piaget outlined a theory of cognitive development where individuals progress through a sequence of invariant stages each reflecting increasingly more sophisticated forms of thought. Piaget stressed the interaction between an individual's level of maturation and the environment where an individual actively constructed knowledge.

Key to Piaget's view of the learning process is the concept of schemas (units of thought which are the result of internalised action) and operations, mental rules of logic.

Vygotsky emphasised the role of language, specifically that language learned in social interactions ultimately makes thought and problem solving possible. Vygotsky sees knowledge as being imparted by the more experienced adult, with the less experienced individual taking on the role of an apprentice.

Bruner, in agreement with Piaget, argues that individuals are born with biological systems that enable them to make sense of their world, but that these systems become increasingly more complex with time. Bruner, like Piaget, believes that individuals need to actively construct knowledge, hence discovery learning. However, more in agreement with Vygotsky, Bruner emphasised the role of language. Language not only reflects learning but under the right circumstances can enhance learning.

Fill in the chart below.

	Key concepts	Role of language	Role of individual in the learning process (i.e. active or passive?)	Role of maturation (When is a child ready to learn?)	Curriculum (What should be taught?)	Teaching styles (How should the curriculum be taught?)
Piaget						
Vygotsky						
Bruner						

Review exercise

Further reading

Wood, D. (1998) *How Children Think and Learn*, 2nd edn, Oxford: Blackwell. Hard-going but very insightful and a useful reference.

Donaldson, M. (1978) *Children's Minds*, London: Fontana. A classic in the field!

2

Perspectives on learning: the behaviourist and humanistic approach

Introduction

In this chapter we will look at how psychologists from a behaviourist and a humanistic background explain the learning process. In addition we will explore how these views have been applied in the classroom.

Behaviourist approach

One of the oldest scientific approaches to studying learning is to concentrate on observable behaviour, thus 'behaviourism'. Learning theory deals with the relationship between stimuli (events in the environment) and subsequent responses made by an individual.

Legendary psychologists such as Watson, Pavlov and Skinner have dominated this field. This approach has been widely criticised and might seem somewhat outdated; however, this theory has led to and will probably continue to lead to many useful applications.

Classical conditioning

When studying salivation responses in dogs, Ivan Pavlov, a Russian physiologist (1849–1936), noticed and described what is now known as classical conditioning theory. What Pavlov observed was a simple fact that any dog owner would know, that dogs salivate not only when food is presented but also when food is about to be presented, i.e. in response to the sound of the tin opener or to their owner's melodic calls of 'come and get it'. From this simple observation Pavlov designed an experimental procedure. Pavlov also coined terminology to explain the process. The experiment goes as follows. The food is the **unconditioned stimulus** eliciting an **unconditioned response** of salivation. If a bell (**conditioned stimulus**) immediately precedes the presentation of food (unconditioned stimulus) then, after several pairings of the bell and the food, the bell (conditioned stimulus) acquires the ability to elicit the **conditioned response** of salivation.

Pavlov's study might just seem like another bizarre story from the annals of psychology but there are important applications. The principles Pavlov outlined can be applied to learned emotional reactions and learned emotional reactions, are central to the educational process.

Example of learned emotional reactions

Connie is a very bright 16-year-old. She achieved ten grade As for her GCSEs, with the exception of maths for which she received a U. Unfortunately Connie's dream is to become a teacher and she needs a pass in GCSE maths. Connie confided to her psychology teacher that she had an unfortunate experience with a teacher in regard to maths when she was 7. One day in class the teacher, a Mrs Maude Ramsbristle, asked her what was five times five. Connie gave the wrong answer and for her transgression had to sit at the back of the class with her face to the wall wearing a strange hat. Connie has hated maths ever since. The psychology teacher felt that Connie had developed a learned emotional reaction to maths and that this could be explained in terms of classical conditioning theory.

How Connie learned to fear maths

Fill in the blanks using the appropriate phrases:

being in a maths class   humiliation   being upset   fear of humiliation.

Unconditioned stimulus (UCS)	elicits	Unconditioned Response (UCR)
(being placed at back of class, told to wear a strange hat . . .)		_____
Conditioned stimulus (CS)	elicits	Conditioned response (CR)
_____		_____

(Answers on p. 00)

Progress exercise 2.1

Evaluation of classical conditioning

A key point is that learning any skill involves many cognitive processes. An individual's motivation to learn and their belief in their ability to learn will affect how they learn. It is essential that learning be a positive experience, as unpleasant emotional associations (such as those described in Progress exercise 2.1) will interfere with the learning process.

Operant conditioning

Operant conditioning states that environmental contingencies or the environment's 'reaction' to an individual's behaviour controls that individual's behaviour. Theorists such as Skinner (1903–1991) state that actions that are followed by reinforcing consequences are more likely to re-occur, and that actions that are followed by unpleasant or punishing consequences are less likely to re-occur. Again this might seem deceptively simple. However, the theory becomes more complicated when one realises that what constitutes punishment and reinforcement differs depending on the individual. Skinner also noted that the situation within which the learning took place had to be taken into account. In analysing and trying to account for behaviour, the psychologist, as behavioural detective, needs to take into account the antecedent (what happens immediately before the behaviour), the behaviour, and the consequences of the behaviour. This method is known as the ABC approach (A for antecedent, B for behaviour and C for consequences).

Skinner further distinguished between positive and negative reinforcement. Both positive and negative reinforcement increase the probability that the response will occur again; however, they act differently upon the individual to create the same effect. With positive reinforcement, a person displays certain behaviour due to the fact that in the past it has led to desirable outcomes. With negative reinforcement, an individual engages in behaviour to avoid a previously experienced negative response.

Example of positive and negative reinforcement

Both Billy and Bob always hand work in on time. The motivation for Bob is the fact that his teacher smiles at him. Bob finds this particularly rewarding. Bob is being positively reinforced for 'handing in' work. Billy on the other hand lives in dread of his teacher and hands in work promptly to avoid her legendary wrath. Billy's 'handing in' behaviour is being negatively reinforced.

The question is which type of reinforcement is more beneficial in the long run?

Schedules of reinforcement

Another factor that Skinner outlined as being important to the learning process was that the schedule of reinforcement made a difference. Behaviour that was rewarded on an intermittent or variable schedule was more resistant to extinction. Do you know anyone who buys lottery tickets? How often do they win? Winning would probably be on a variable interval schedule, that is, some weeks an individual might win £10, but then they might go for weeks or months without winning any money. As the reward for buying lottery tickets is on a variable interval schedule such behaviour is difficult to extinguish, or in other words difficult to stop.

Shaping

Skinner further noted that complex behaviour could be broken into smaller component parts and that these component parts could be selectively reinforced. The process of selectively reinforcing more and more component parts of a complex skill is called shaping.

Evaluation of operant conditioning

Skinner's theory of conditioning was built upon laboratory experiments with animals such as pigeons and rats. Skinner was interested in establishing general learning principles. One criticism involves the extent to which research based on animals can be applied to people. It has also been argued that this approach takes a mechanistic view of humanity and sees individuals as robotic slaves to the environmental consequences of their actions. The realisation that tangible and observable rewards were not necessary for learning to take place led psychologists, in the 1960s, to look at other theories such as that of Piaget. Learning theory does not take into account hidden, unobservable cognitive and emotional factors involved in learning. This can be considered as both a weakness and a strength. There are some instances where it is not possible to ask an individual what they think or how they feel, and in these cases analysis of behaviour can lead to successful interventions and educational strategies.

Applications of behaviourism

Skinner believed that behaviour was controlled by environmental contingencies – that is, the likelihood that a person would repeat a certain unit of behaviour in the future depended on the consequences of exhibiting the behaviour in the past. Reinforcement would increase the likelihood of repeating the behaviour while punishment would decrease the likelihood of repeating the behaviour.

Skinner was interested in applying principles of learning to the classroom. Various forms of reward and punishment exist in the classroom. For example, in the early years children get stickers and stars when they complete their work. In secondary schools there are usually systems of merit points. These would all constitute rewards. In terms of punishment there is the good old detention, standing outside the head's office, suspension and exclusion. Beyond these intuitive uses of learning theory what Skinner was concerned with was whether the principles of learning were being effectively used to promote learning.

One application of learning theory in the classroom would see the teacher analysing the disruptive behaviour of a student in terms of antecedents, behaviour and consequences, in the hope of determining both an explanation for the behaviour and a way forward.

An example of analysing behaviour

Mrs Moody teaches year 3. Mrs Moody's problem is Johnny Smith. Johnny never remains in his seat. He is constantly wandering around the class disrupting the lesson. He crawls under the tables. He jumps on the tables. Yesterday he brought a spider into the class and put it down Samantha Johnson's jumper. Needless to say Samantha was hysterical. Mrs Moody is at her wits' end. She asks another teacher, Mrs Peabody, to come in and observe Johnny, recording his disruptive behaviour in terms of antecedents (what happens before the disruptive behaviour), the behaviour and the consequences of the behaviour. To

Table 2.1 An example of behavioural analysis

Antecedent	Behaviour	Consequence
10:05 Johnny sitting by himself. No one talking to him. Teacher busy at other table.	10:07 Johnny deliberately falls over in his chair and groans loudly: 'Miss, the chair is attacking me.'	10:08 All the children laugh. Teacher says: 'Not again, come over here and sit beside me.'
10:33 Johnny sitting by himself. No one is talking to him. Teacher is busy at other table.	10:34 Johnny starts crawling under the tables pretending he is a dog and barking very loudly.	10:35 All the children laugh and teacher says: 'That's it Johnny, if you can't sit quietly by yourself and do your work, then you will have to sit with me.'

Mrs Moody's surprise an interesting pattern emerges. The observations are outlined in Table 2.1.

What became apparent to Mrs Moody and Mrs Peabody was that Johnny always misbehaved when he was being ignored. An analysis of the records seemed to suggest that the attention he received from the other children and the teacher was positively reinforcing his disruptive behaviour. What Mrs Moody needed to do was to change the environmental contingencies, so that Johnny was being reinforced by attention when he was actually behaving.

Skinner was opposed to the use of aversive methods, such as punishment, in the classroom, for while aversive methods tell an individual what not to do they do not tell an individual what they should do. Skinner argued for the utilisation at all times of positive reinforcement in shaping desired responses. Returning to our example of Johnny, Mrs Moody too thought that perhaps shaping of appropriate behaviour would be a suitable way forward. Below Mrs Moody outlines her planned intervention.

Example of an intervention involving shaping

Mrs Moody: 'What Johnny needs is attention and lots of it. The plan is to reward appropriate behaviour with attention and to ignore disruptive behaviour. What I want you to do is to record how long Johnny sits quietly at his desk. If he manages to sit there for two minutes without doing anything disruptive you are to go over to him and say how well he is behaving.'

Classroom assistant: 'You mean even if Johnny is not doing any work, but just sitting there, I am to praise him?'

Mrs Moody: 'Yes. In shaping of appropriate behaviour we have to start with an analysis of what constitutes appropriate behaviour. Right now Johnny doesn't sit at his desk. In this case sitting at a desk quietly and working has to be broken into its component parts. The component parts are: sitting at his desk, sitting at his desk for a stipulated amount of time, sitting at his desk and working, sitting and working at his desk for a stipulated length of time. This week we will concentrate on him just sitting quietly. Then gradually we will require him to sit quietly for longer and then we will require him to actually sit there and do work. This should work in time.'

Evaluation of applications

Skinner believed that reinforcers in school were administered without the due consideration needed to make learning most effective.

One of Skinner's most useful applications in classroom practice was strategies that involve the teacher in consciously analysing the behaviour of the students. However, this approach takes time and involves careful observation and record keeping.

Skinner believed that children need to be active in the learning process, not for the reasons Piaget or Bruner would give, but that they need to be active in order to receive constant evaluation and reinforcement. This is not always achievable in a large classroom where the teacher's attention may be focused on a few students at any one time.

Skinner was also concerned with the concept of whole class teaching in that this would mean that the teacher would concentrate on the average student whilst ignoring the individual needs of the slower or more able students. Skinner believed that the way forward was with teaching machines. His teaching machine would allow individuals to progress at their own rate; it could transmit basic information and therefore free the teacher for meaningful exchanges. Skinner created some crude teaching machines, which he used in his own teaching. However, they were cumbersome and expensive and never caught on (Richelle 1993). The advent of modern personal computers creates the perfect medium for the type of programmed learning that Skinner envisioned.

In terms of teaching the curriculum, Skinner felt that teachers needed to be clear regarding what is taught, to have clear objectives, to teach first things first and to allow students to progress at their own rate.

One area, which proved controversial, was Skinner's belief in errorless learning – that is, that a programme should avoid the possibility of the individual experiencing failure. Others have argued that this does not reflect the real world and that it is important that students learn to cope with failure and set-backs positively.

Let's suppose you wish to design an educational programme for 7-year-olds to learn multiplication. Your boss wants you to design a game with armies of Jedi knights pitted against hordes of horrific space octopuses. Using a framework provided by learning theory, what would you do?

(Hint: use the terminology – for example, positive reinforcement and shaping.)

Progress exercise 2.2

Humanistic approach

Humanistic psychology is said to be in direct opposition to behaviourism. The rationale for this argument is that inasmuch as behaviourism focuses on observable behaviour, humanism focuses on the unobservable private mental world of an individual. In the following section we will look at humanistic theories and specifically how these views are translated into classroom practice.

Rogers

Carl Ransom Rogers (1902–1989) is credited with being one of the founding fathers of the humanistic movement. Rogers created a new type of therapy, which was non-directive and client-centred. But what do these terms mean? Rogers believed that:

- As our worlds are highly private, behaviour can only be understood from the individual's point of view. Individuals interpret experiences in their own unique way. We might know what has happened for another person but we do not know how the individual has interpreted these experiences. Hence the expression: 'How was it for you?'
- The goal of human existence is self-actualisation. (Self-actualisation is to become all that we are capable of becoming.)
- We can endeavour to understand another through a special type of relationship. (Rogers argued that an individual needs to feel valued

and prized by a therapist who communicates to the client warmth, empathy and acceptance. When a client feels this acceptance, the client can begin to explore their own inner experiences in a safe environment. Through a self-exploration of their internal world the client can move towards self-actualisation. In this sense Rogers' therapy is non-directive and client-centred, in that it gives control to the client.)

(LeFrancois 1997, Kirschenbaum and
Land Henderson 1990)

Kirschenbaum and Land Henderson (1990) argue that Rogers' views on teaching are a natural extension of his views in regard to therapy. Rogers (1957) offers the following personal reflections on teaching:

- 'It seems to me that anything that can be taught to another is relatively inconsequential and has little or no significant influence on behaviour' (p. 302).
- 'I have come to feel that the only learning which significantly influences behaviour is self-discovered, self-appropriated learning' (p. 302).
- 'Such experience would imply that we would do away with teaching. People would get together if they wished to learn' (p. 303).
- 'We would do away with examinations. They measure only the inconsequential type of learning' (p. 303).
- 'We would do away with grades and credits for the same reason' (p. 303).
- 'We would do away with degrees . . . a degree marks an end or a conclusion of something, and a learner is only interested in the continuing process of learning' (p. 303).

It is important to stress that these are personal reflections and that even Rogers conceded that these reflections might seem fantastic. However, perhaps what Rogers was interested in was opening a debate on what learning was, what real learning felt like and what learning should strive to be.

Rogers' views on education developed over time and in 1977 he wrote an article in which he contrasted the traditional mode of teaching with a more person-centered approach. A traditional mode of teaching would include views favoured by the behaviourist approach.

Table 2.2 A comparison between traditional and person-centred modes of teaching

	Traditional mode	Person-centred mode
Relationship between teacher and student	The teacher is the possessor of knowledge; the student receives the knowledge.	The teacher is secure within themselves and their relationship with their students, and from this relationship has a firm belief in the students' capacity to learn for themselves.
Teaching style	The lecture or textbooks are the means by which the teacher imparts knowledge.	The teacher shares with the students the responsibility for learning.
Teaching environment	• The teacher is the possessor of power and it is the student's role to obey. • Trust is at a minimum. • The emphasis is on authority. • Students are governed by being kept in an intermittent or constant state of fear. • Democracy and its values are ignored in practice. • There is no place for the whole person.	• Students alone or in groups develop their own programme of learning. • A learning climate is provided which encourages personal growth. • Emphasis is placed on the continuing process of learning.
Evaluation	Examinations measure the extent to which the student has internalised the required knowledge.	The learner primarily makes the evaluation of learning.

Applications of the humanistic approach

Again this is all very heady stuff. But the question remains as to exactly how this humanistic approach is translated into the classroom.

Kirschenbaum (1975) comments on the difficulty of defining exactly what humanistic education is. This difficulty stems from the fact that humanistic education is in fact an umbrella term that refers to several related approaches. These approaches can be classified as:

1 **Humanistic Content Curricula**: here the curriculum is deemed as relevant to the students' lives (for example, drug awareness); therefore the curriculum is humanistic though it could be taught in a traditional format.
2 **Humanistic Process Curricula**: here the curriculum involves focusing on the whole student and teaching the student life skills (for example, assertiveness training) which the student will need to be a more effective and whole person.
3 **Humanistic School and Group Structures**: this approach implies restructuring the school or learning environment so that humanistic aims can be pursued.

- On a whole school level this approach could imply having such features as open classrooms, class meetings, and finding alternative systems to evaluation.
- On a class level this approach would advocate the following:

  (a) Students being able to exercise choice and control over educational and daily activities.
  (b) The curriculum would focus on felt concerns, that is, what the individuals deemed as important to learn.
  (c) A focus on life skills. This would involve integrating thinking skills with personal skills such as sharing and communicating effectively. A possible example of this would be certain components of co-operative learning.
  (d) The student would be involved in self-evaluation and would monitor their own progress to their own personally set goals.
  (e) The teacher would take on the role of a facilitator. A facilitator's role is to be supportive and genuine. The teacher, as facilitator, while having a role in the learning process, does not control the learning process and can be seen as a learner inasmuch as the students are.

Examples of Humanistic Process Curricula

Co-operative learning

Johnson *et al.* (1984) outline four components in regard to co-operative learning:

- *'Positive interdependence'* whereby students work towards attaining a common goal and sharing materials.
- *'Individual accountability'* which implies that every student must contribute to the final outcome.
- *'Interpersonal and small-group skill development'* which has a social skill objective as part of the group learning process.
- *'Face-to-Face Interactions'* which are an essential part of this learning strategy.

An example of co-operative learning technique

Mrs Smart has divided her Year 5 class into groups of five. The task for each group is to act out a favourite nursery rhyme or fairy tale and to perform this play at the school assembly. The task itself is divided into various roles which include: writing the play; sending out invitations; making costumes; and keeping a work diary. Each child is assigned a role and in that regard each child is dependent on the others. By keeping a work diary and documenting who does what, each child becomes accountable to the others. The social skill task for this group assignment is to become good listeners and to praise each other. The teacher asks the group to record what suggestions each person made in regard to what they should do, in the following way: '_____ suggested that we do _____. We thought this would be funny _____, interesting _____, a good idea but too difficult _____.'

(Children are required to tick one of the above.)

In this group activity there are many opportunities for face-to-face interaction.

EVALUATION OF CO-OPERATIVE LEARNING

There is much evidence for the value of this approach. Many see this approach as balancing the need to teach and achieve academic skills with the need to acquire personal and life skills (Snow and Swanson 1992, Johnson and Johnson 1994). Furthermore this technique has been found to be effective in including children with disabilities in mainstream classrooms (Putnam 1993).

Emotional literacy classes

One recent application within the humanistic framework is the advent of emotional literacy classes. Goleman (1996) outlines the importance of emotional intelligence and describes the advent and benefits of self science or emotional literacy classes. This approach, instead of acknowledging the role of emotions and feelings in learning, aims to teach emotional skills. Goleman (1996) claims that such emotional literacy programmes improve children's academic achievement scores. The content of such programmes would include: emotional self-awareness; managing emotions; harnessing emotions productively; reading emotions; and handling relationships. In arguing for a need for such classes Goleman (1996) states:

> In a time when too many children lack the capacity to handle their upsets, to listen or focus, to rein in impulse, to feel responsible for their work or care about learning, anything that will buttress these skills will help in their education. In this sense, emotional literacy enhances schools' ability to teach.
>
> (p. 284)

Progress exercise 2.3

In the previous example in this chapter of Mrs Moody and Johnny Smith (see pages 26–27), Mrs Moody attempted to explain Johnny's disruptive behaviour and to find possible ways forward within a behaviourist framework. How would Rogers interpret Johnny's disruptive behaviour and what would be the possible ways forward according to the humanistic approach?

Evaluation of humanistic approaches

The humanistic approach is said to be ambiguous, vague and woolly. The students might be learning what they want and having fun but are they learning what they need to learn? Of course the question then is who defines what students need to learn? In a world where skills and academic competencies are valued, the question remains as to whether the humanistic approach effectively teaches competencies. But as we have seen, a humanistic approach can mean many things. A humanistic approach can apply to the content of the curriculum, a method of teaching or a particular interpersonal style of the teacher. Although the teaching approaches advocated by theorists such as Skinner, Piaget, Bruner, Vygotsky and Rogers might seem very different, in reality a teacher can pick and choose various approaches to suit individual students and particular lessons. The fact that teachers can use a combination of approaches makes it difficult to determine which approach is the most effective.

Summary

The behaviourist approach to learning focuses on observable behaviour, rather than hidden, unobservable cognitive factors. A classical conditioning view of learning highlights the importance of conditioned emotional responses. Operant conditioning sees behaviour as being controlled by environmental contingencies. According to the theory the likelihood of a person engaging in any given behaviour depends on the past consequences of that behaviour, that is, whether that behaviour was punished or reinforced. Two useful applications of operant conditioning include an ABC (antecedent, behaviour, and consequences) analysis of behaviour and shaping of appropriate behaviour.

In contrast, the humanistic approach focuses on hidden internal experiences and emphasises that the role of feelings must be acknowledged and incorporated into the learning experience. Two examples of applications within the humanistic approach are co-operative learning and emotional literacy classes.

Review exercise		Key concepts	Role of individual in the learning process (i.e. active or passive?)	Curriculum (What should be taught?)	Teaching styles (How should the curriculum be taught?)
	Skinner				
	Rogers				

Further reading

Kirschenbaum, H. and Land Henderson, V. (eds) (1990) *The Carl Rogers Reader*, London: Constable. This book contains a very interesting chapter on education, which contains selections from Rogers' published work.

Richelle, M.N. (1993) *B.F. Skinner: A Reappraisal*, Hove: Erlbaum. This book contains a very useful chapter outlining Skinner's contribution to education.

3

Assessing educational performance

Introduction

A starting point for this chapter will be to address the issue of why educators, teachers and theorists are interested in assessing educational performance. Presumably there must be a reason, there must be advantages, or is it, as a cynical student might say, just a cruel and unusual form of punishment?

Assessment can take many forms. There are intelligence tests, ability tests, the national Standard Assessment Tests (SATs) and of course informal class tests. Much has been said regarding the limitations of assessment. Some will argue that intelligence is such an abstract concept that it cannot adequately be measured. Others will state that forms of assessment such as the SATs have led to a competitive atmosphere between schools. In this chapter we will strive for a balanced approach, acknowledging both the benefits to be gained and the existing limitations in regard to assessing educational performance. This chapter will also attempt to find a balance between explaining theoretical concepts relating to assessment and illustrating how these concepts have been applied.

What is psychometrics?

The term psychometrics has two meanings. In the first instance it can refer to any form of mental testing. For example, this could include testing or assessment of various personality measures (including learning style inventories), establishing indexes of intelligence or determining aptitudes for people entering various professions. In the second instance psychometrics refers to the application of principles of mathematics and statistics to the data of psychology (Reber 1985). These principles of mathematics and statistics are important as they can be used to evaluate various assessment methods used in teaching. These principles include:

- *Norming*: norming involves giving a test to a representative sample of individuals and on the basis of their results establishing various levels of performance – for example, what scores indicate a grade A, what scores indicate a grade B, etc.
- *Reliability*: reliability refers to consistency of measurement. Consistency can be looked at from several perspectives:

  (a) Test–retest refers to the degree to which an individual's score on one occasion is related to their score on another occasion.
  (b) The degree of similarity between tests, or alternative forms of tests, which aim to measure the same construct.
  (c) The extent to which markers agree with each other when grading a test.
  (d) The extent to which a rater or marker's grading remains consistent over a marking period.
  (e) Internal consistency of test. This measure is attained by comparing scores on one half of the test with those on the other half of the test. This is known as split-half reliability.

- *Validity*: validity refers to the extent to which a test actually measures the trait it is claiming to measure. This is often referred to as construct validity. Construct validity can be divided into content validity and predictive validity. Predictive validity assesses the extent to which the measurement device or test can be used to make future inferences. For example, on the basis of an IQ test result, inferences could be made about future academic successes. Content validity measures the extent to which a test on a specific domain of knowledge, for example a test on the history of ancient Egypt, actually measures that domain of knowledge. If someone scored highly on this test how much would they really know about the history of ancient Egypt?

- *Item analysis*: specific items on tests can be analysed in terms of how many students answered each question correctly or incorrectly. Items can also be checked for any form of bias (Corsini and Auerbach 1996).

Mr Wise, head of history, gives all Year 8 students a test on the Tudors, which comprises fifty multiple-choice questions and three essay questions. Mr Wise wrote the test himself. Students in Year 8 are divided into four ability groups with a different teacher teaching each ability group. The individual teachers mark the tests.

- How can the principles of mathematics and statistics be applied to Mr Wise's history test?

(Hint: you will need to consider the concepts of norming, various forms of reliability, validity and item analysis.)

Progress exercise 3.1

Types of psychometric tests

IQ tests

Binet and Simon developed the first IQ test in 1905. Their aim was to devise an objective test, which would measure intelligence. It was hoped that on the basis of this test they would be able to differentiate between: children who could be educated within the public school system; those children who would need special education; and those who were deemed ineducable and in need of institutionalisation. The test achieved its aims, and subsequent tests succeeded in being able to differentiate abilities within these three groups of children.

From these small beginnings emerged the big business of intelligence or mental ability testing. Historically, IQ or intelligence quotient is calculated by the following formula:

MA (mental age) ÷ CA (chronological/biological age) × 100 = IQ

If a child of 10 has a mental age of 12 then their IQ is 120

12/10 × 100 = 120

More recently IQ has been calculated by comparing a child's performance with a large group of children of the same age (norming). However, a score of 100 is still defined as average (Bee 1989).

Table 3.1 shows the labels given to individuals according to their IQ scores: 67 per cent of the population will have IQ scores ranging from 85 to 115, with 96 per cent of the population having IQ scores ranging from 70 to 130.

Table 3.1 **Labels given to individuals according to their IQ scores**

IQ	Description
Above 130	Very superior
120–129	Superior
110–119	High average
90–109	Average
80–89	Low average
70–79	Borderline
55–69	Mild learning disabilities
40–54	Moderate learning disabilities
25–39	Severe learning disabilities
0–24	Profound learning disabilities

Source: Adapted from Atkinson *et al.* 1993.

The assumption behind intelligence tests is that there is a general mental ability (g) which underlies performance on many different types of tests. However it is also believed that alongside this general ability there are specific abilities (s) which can influence certain types of tasks. 'Thus in any intelligent act, "g"' is involved, plus the "s" factor or factors appropriate to that particular act' (Fontana 1995, p. 103).

A key point in regard to intelligence tests is that they aim to measure underlying ability in regard to intelligence and not the products of specific learning programmes. Attainment tests, such as National Curriculum tests, measure the outcomes, or knowledge demonstrated, after specific programmes of instruction. Intelligence tests attempt to measure abilities, which reflect experience but are not specifically taught as part of the school curriculum.

The Wechsler scales

One of the most widely used IQ tests in this country is the Wechsler scales. The Wechsler IQ test is an example of an individual test – that is, a psychologist administers the test to an individual student. The Wechsler IQ scales comprise two scales, verbal and performance. Each scale is made up of a number of sub-tests (Salvia and Ysseldyke 1998). The verbal scale measures performance on sub-tests such as vocabulary and comprehension, which are presented verbally, while the performance scale requires the individual to physically manipulate or arrange blocks, pictures or other materials.

Cognitive ability tests

Cognitive ability tests (CATs) are an example of a group test, that is, paper-and-pencil tests which are administered to many individuals at one point in time (Thorndike *et al*. 1986). The CATs are aimed at students in Years 3 to 11. The CATs measure abilities in specific areas:

- *Verbal reasoning* is measured by 'fill in the blank' questions such as: 'The book was not very _____. I fell asleep reading it.' The student is required to choose from the following words:

  exciting boring sad hungry.

Table 3.2 The Wechsler IQ test

Verbal scale	*Performance scale*
• *Information and comprehension*: understanding of social rules and concepts. Examples of a question given would be: 'How many eyes do you have?' and 'Why do people wear boots after it snows?'	• *Picture completion* (the ability to detect missing parts of pictures, such as a door handle missing from a door)
• *Arithmetic* (test of mental arithmetic)	• *Picture arrangement* (the individual is required to re-arrange sets of pictures to express a meaningful story)
• *Similarities* (a test of verbal reasoning. For example: 'In what way are an apple and a banana alike?')	• *Block design* (a construction test involving the manipulation of cubes to match two-dimensional patterns)
• *Vocabulary* (this measures an individual's ability to define words. For example: 'What is meant by the word diamond?')	• *Object assembly* (a jigsaw-type task)
• *Digit span* (a test of short-term memory capacity)	• *Coding* (involves drawing an appropriate symbol or digit to match a shape)

- *Quantitative reasoning* involves the use of numbers and symbols. This scale indicates potential achievement in science and mathematics. For example, a student might be asked to indicate how two number concepts are related. The question might be: 'Is one pound equal to, greater than, or less than 75 pennies?'

- *Non-verbal reasoning* involves manipulation of geometric or spatial elements without verbal influences. The student might be asked to complete the sequence illustrated in Figure 3.1.

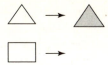

Figure 3.1 **Example of non-verbal reasoning**

Value of psychometric tests

- *Diagnosis of specific need*: a score of below 70 on a standardised intelligence test (i.e. Wechsler) would suggest global learning disabilities. An IQ of less than 70 will usually result in a statement of special educational need and a placement in a special school. An uneven performance on various sub-tests could indicate specific learning disabilities. For example, a dyslexic child might be of average or above-average ability on picture completion, picture arrangement, comprehension and vocabulary, but considerably below average on digit span and coding (Thomson 1990).
- *Referral for intervention*: schools use the results from CATs for target setting. If a student fails to reach these targets, then under-achievement is indicated and intervention is needed.
- *Setting/streaming*: a school uses CAT scores for streaming, that is, organising students in similar-ability groups.
- *Value of individual and group tests*: as the Wechsler is an individual test, which is verbally given, the test has advantages. The individual's responses to test items are not reliant on their ability to read the questions or write down the answers. As the CATs are a group test, schools can administer the test to large groups of students and use the results to provide information for target setting and streaming.
- *Dynamic testing*: Raven's Progressive Matrices, a popular ability test, has been used for 'dynamic testing', that is, not only to establish what a person's ability is, but to establish potential ability. The Raven's Progressive Matrices test was given to a group of five New Deal clients, individuals who had dropped out of education and who had never held down a job. The New Deal clients after completing the test were taught a general procedure to help them work out the answers. Then these same individuals were given an alternative version of the test. After instruction all five clients scored perfect

results, compared to their original scores of between 50 and 75 per cent. These results reflect those of similar studies carried out on students. The implications of 'dynamic testing' are that it presents a method that would enable future employers or teachers to gauge not only present ability but also potential to learn (Pickard 1998).

Limitations of psychometric tests

- *Validity*: it has been argued that a test that sees intelligence as a global entity and measures general cognitive performance will not give an accurate picture of what an individual does know. Miller-Jones (1989) argues from the position of cultural practice theory and a contextual analysis of cognitive performance. What he is saying is that learning is acquired within a specific context or environment and is not necessarily generalised to other contexts. An example that is often given is that adults can undertake in supermarkets context-related mathematical calculations that they could not do in a more formal school environment (Cumming and Maxwell 1999).

- *Reliability*: modern psychometric tests spend considerable time establishing reliability indexes. Internal consistency is measured by split-half reliability. Test scores do vary due to other factors, which will be discussed under the heading of performance versus ability.

- *Performance versus ability*: intuitively we know that there is a difference between what we do know, our ability, and how we express this ability to others, that is, how well we perform on the day of the test. There are various factors that will affect our performance:

  (i) *Comprehension of the questions*. The fact that the CAT is a written test will mean that performance depends on the individual student being able to read and understand the questions.

  (ii) *Tester variables*. The fact that the Wechsler scales are an individual test presents some possible difficulties. In an individual test, the tester's behaviour becomes an important factor in regard to the individual's performance. Perhaps the tester is seen as intimidating, resulting in a lower score. Perhaps the tester gives subtle hints at desired responses by inadvertent body language, such as directing his or her eye gaze to the correct response; this would result in a higher score (Fontana 1995).

(iii) *Expectations regarding test performance.* An individual's belief in their ability will affect their performance.

(iv) *Motivation to complete the test.* An individual's desire to do well will influence their performance.

(v) *Socio-economic factors.* Research has shown that mean IQ increases with socio-economic status, but why this is so is not clear (Fontana 1995). There are many possible reasons for such a relationship. Families from higher socio-economic groups can provide resources such as computers, internet access and books. Such families can pay for private tuition if their child is struggling in a certain area. Perhaps such families offer more complex and stimulating environments. Maybe such parents act as powerful role models.

- *Gender issues*: there are no important sex differences in overall intelligence test scores; however, differences do appear for specific abilities. Males typically score higher on visual-spatial measures and, beginning in middle childhood, score higher on mathematical tests. Females excel on a number of verbal measures (APA 1996).

- *Issues regarding ethnic groups*: much controversy surrounds the issue of differences in IQ scores across different ethnic groups. There have been criticisms regarding whether IQ tests are culturally fair. Modern IQ tests have struggled to eliminate such biases. It is also argued that IQ tests are culturally bound, that is they reflect a Western view of intelligence. However, even within Western societies there are differences in IQ scores between ethnic groups. Although individuals from all ethnic groups can be seen at all levels of IQ, the mean IQ of white Americans is higher than that of black Americans. The APA (1996) report that this result is not due to differences in socio-economic status or to obvious biases in test construction. Further they state that there is no evidence to support a genetic interpretation for these findings, but the reason for such differences is not known. In a discussion of such differences it is crucial to recall what IQ tests actually measure. Neisser (1997, p. 1) states that IQ tests 'tap certain abilities that are relevant to success in school and do so with remarkable consistency. On the other hand, many significant cognitive traits – creativity, wisdom, practical sense, social sensitivity – are obviously beyond their reach.'

In summary, ability tests by themselves do not provide all the answers, but they are a useful starting point. It is always advised that ability tests in combination with other forms of assessment be used when making educational decisions.

Types of performance assessment at different ages: the National Curriculum and Key Stages

The Education Reform Act (1988) and the Education Act (1996) state that all children who attend state schools within England and Wales must be taught according to the National Curriculum. The National Curriculum is an encompassing document outlining what subjects should be taught at what ages and what levels of attainment should be achieved. Table 3.3 outlines some basic details concerning the National Curriculum.

The National Curriculum is incredibly detailed in that, for each subject, it outlines areas to be covered, with specific attainment goals. Let's take the example of science. Table 3.4 outlines how an individual topic is taught and assessed at Key Stage 1.

What Table 3.4 illustrates is the amount of detail that the National Curriculum covers, in terms of both subject content and assessment criteria. In terms of attainment levels, the comments listed in Table 3.4 are only some of the guidelines given.

We have mentioned that there are national standardised tests at the end of each key stage, but we also know from personal experience that much more assessment goes on within schools above and beyond the nationalised tests.

Specific ways in which educational performance can be assessed

Before we examine the variety of assessment options available to a teacher, it is helpful to define a few terms.

- *Formative assessment* refers to daily ongoing feedback, which the teacher gives to the student to assist learning.

Table 3.3 The National Curriculum: Key Stages

Key Stage	Age	Year group	Subjects taught	Attainment levels	Assessment
Key Stage 1	5–7	1–2	English, Maths, Science, ICT, Design and Technology, History, Geography, Art and Design, Music, PE, Religious Education	Within ranges 1–3	End of key stage assessment, SATs (English, Maths and Science) and Teacher assessments.
Key Stage 2	7–11	3–6	Same as Key Stage 1	Within ranges 2–5	Same as for Key Stage 1
Key Stage 3	11–14	7–9	Same as Key Stages 1 and 2 with addition of modern foreign language and sex education.	Within ranges 3–8; 8 is available for the very able student	Same as for Key Stages 1 and 2
Key Stage 4	14–16	10–11	English, Maths, Science, Design and Technology, ICT, Physical Education and Sex Education	Scale does not apply	GCSE

Table 3.4 'Science: Life Processes and Living Things, Green Plants as Organisms'

Key Stage	Programme of Study	Levels of Attainment Assessment Criteria
Key Stage 1	(a) that plants need light and water to grow; (b) to recognise and name the leaf, flower, stem and root of the flowering plants; (c) that flowering plants grow and produce seeds which in turn produce new plants. (p. 4)	**Level 1** Students recognise and name external parts of plants, using words such as leaf or flower. They observe and describe a range of plants in terms of features such as colour or leaf size. **Level 2** Students use their knowledge to describe basic conditions such as supply of water, food, air or light that plants need in order to survive. They can sort living things into groups based on simple features. **Level 3** Students use their knowledge of growth or reproduction when they describe differences between living and non-living things. They provide simple explanations for changes in living things, such as how water or the lack of light may alter plant growth.

Source: Adapted from the National Curriculum 1995.

- *Summative assessment* can be seen as a snapshot of an individual's educational abilities at a given point in time.
- *Norm-referenced assessment* involves placing individuals on a scale in relation to other individuals' performance on a certain task. This process allows for individual comparison. An example of norm-referenced assessment would be any test which gives individual scores, such as an IQ test or an A level exam.
- *Criterion-referenced assessment* allows for comparisons with others, but students doing this type of test would have to meet all designated criteria or achieve learning outcomes to a set standard in order to pass. An example of criterion-referenced assessment would be a driving test. Another example would be some GNVQ or NVQ courses where the syllabus is written in such a way that students need to show evidence of achieving all specified learning outcomes in order to gain a pass.

Tables 3.5 and 3.6 outline various methods of assessment with advantages and disadvantages (cited and adapted from Clarke 1998).

One of the outcomes from Key Stage 1, 'Science: Life Processes and Living Things' is 'to recognise and name the leaf, flower, stem and root of the flowering plants'.

- Suggest three ways to assess the outcomes and, for each, give one advantage and one disadvantage.

Progress exercise 3.2

Value and limitations of assessment

Validity and authentic assessment

One limitation of assessment concerns whether the assessment has validity. A recent way of approaching the concept of validity is to focus on whether the assessment task is a true indicator of the achievement of intended learned outcomes. Central to this issue has been a recent

Table 3.5 Summative assessment

Method of Assessment	Advantages	Disadvantages
International and national tests	• International tests allow comparisons between countries. This can point out areas in need of improvement. • National tests allows comparisons between pupils and schools. • From such results targets can be set. For example, the government has set a target that 75% of children should reach at least level 4 at Key Stage 2.	• Such comparisons may not be valid. • Publication of league tables may lead to unnecessary competition. • National tests may result in teaching to the test. • League tables may not tell the entire story.
National non-statutory tests voluntarily administered in years between SAT tests	• Opportunity to keep track of an individual's progress.	
Baseline tests	• Establish a child's ability at the beginning of their schooling. This can serve as a point from which future progress can be determined. This data would be	• A value added component could be added to the information given out in league tables.

	necessary to calculate the value added index, which denotes the extent of an individual's progress.	• Parents may choose to send their children to schools whose pupils experienced the greatest progress.
Commercially produced tests e.g. Neale Analysis of Reading Ability	• Allow teachers and schools to monitor progress between key stages. • Standardised tests with details regarding age norms.	• Must be purchased.
School tests In-house tests written by teachers to assess end of module attainment.	• Enable teachers to establish attainment levels and track progress.	• Issues of validity and reliability. • Issue of whether performance adequately reflects ability.
Day-to-day class tests	• Enable teachers to track progress. • Necessitate that students revise material.	• Issues of validity and reliability.
End of key stage teacher assessment Teacher decides on attainment level using descriptions and professional judgement.	• Cross-check that could be used as an index of validity regarding the end of key stage assessments.	• If there is a discrepancy between teacher assessment and SAT score it is difficult to ascertain the reason why. Is it due to teacher's misinterpretation of attainment levels or factors that affected student performance in the SATs?

Table 3.6 Formative assessment

Method of assessment	Advantages	Disadvantages
Sharing learning intentions This could be done per lesson.	• Student and pupil both know what is expected. • Encourages both to keep focused on task. • Encourages student involvement.	• Students will know when the teacher, for whatever reason, has not covered all the learning objectives.
Pupil self-evaluation Students are trained to measure or evaluate their own achievement in relation to set learning outcomes.	• Empowers the student. • The student is actively involved in reflecting on his or her own learning activity. • If the student has not achieved the set outcome, the student will need to say why, and this would give the teacher a greater perspective and understanding of the student's viewpoint.	• Assumes that students are motivated to measure their achievement and evaluate their successes. • If learning outcomes are unrealistic for the individual student, the student might get fed up with filling in yet another form to explain 'why I haven't achieved'.

Marking
Could be oral or written. Must be focused on learning outcomes.

- Tracks progress.
- Informs students of their strengths and weaknesses.
- Provides future targets.
- There is an art to marking. If marking is to communicate what was done well, what areas need to be improved and explanations in regard to how to improve, then this takes much time and thought.

Target setting
Students are involved in setting their own individual targets per subject area.

- Student involvement should lead to increased motivation.
- Targets need to be realistic, otherwise students will experience failure which could be anything but motivating.

Records of achievement
Collection of best work.

- This can be seen as a celebration of the student's achievements.
- Documents progress.
- There is an issue of whether this record is shared with the student or is kept as a record of student performance.

focus on what has been described as contextualised and authentic assessment. The call for authentic assessment results from the awareness that many students felt that success in school was trivial, meaningless and contrived (Newmann and Archbald 1992). Wiggins (1993) argues for assessments that better replicate authentic challenges and conditions. Wiggins (1993) calls for 'authentic assessment' to replace isolated drill exercises. Perhaps you have noticed that many questions in textbooks are related to real life events. This is where we come back to the concept of validity. Cumming and Maxwell (1999) argue that in the pursuit of making assessment authentic there can be confusion between what they term first and second order effects. First order expectations relate to the key outcomes, while second order effects relate to other concepts that the student needs to know in order to answer the question. These second order effects are often related to the authentic manner in which the question is phrased. Take the following case study.

Case study

The teacher of Year 6 covering the topic, 'The Victorians', gives the following assignment:

Write two newspaper articles on factory reform. One of these articles will be written from the point of view of the factory owner and one will be written from the point of view of the worker.

In analysis, this assignment could be seen as realistic and interesting but there are first and second order effects. The first order effects would measure what the student knows of life in the factory and factory reform. These are the required outcomes.

Second order effects would involve the students' knowledge of how a newspaper article is written, their ability to write a newspaper article, and their knowledge of how a person who is the owner would write such an article and how the factory worker would write such an article. Realistically a factory worker at that time would probably not be able to write. Perhaps more able students would write an article from the perspective of a social reformer who was interested in the plight of factory workers.

The point is, how well a student performs on this task will depend on their skills in relation to first and second order effects. This could

---

influence the validity of the assignment and, as Cumming and Maxwell (1999, p. 187) state, 'it is all too easy for both the student and the teacher to miss the point of the task. That is, it is all too easy for the second-order expectations to overwhelm the first-order – a case of the medium becoming the message.'

International comparisons

Assessments can offer the possibility of international comparisons. International comparisons have both value and limitations.

International comparisons in regard to achievement have been criticised on several dimensions. It has been argued that perhaps differing levels of achievement merely reflect what curriculum is set for certain age groups. Perhaps what differs between countries is the age at which certain concepts are taught? However, a careful analysis of international comparisons can yield much useful information as the next example will show.

*'England's performance in the Third International Mathematics and
Science Study' (Keys 1997)*

England with over forty other countries participated in an international study on maths and science. The outcome of the study was a league table of countries in regard to achievement in maths and science for 9- and 13-year-olds. England's results were unusual in that achievement in science for both age groups was considerably higher than in maths. The article states:

the key question raised by the results of TIMSS for educators and policy-makers in England are: why did students in England perform relatively well in science but relatively badly in mathematics? The mathematics and science tests were taken by the same children in the same schools and at the primary level, the majority were taught both subjects by the same teacher: why, then should teachers who are relatively successful in teaching science be less successful at teaching mathematics.

(Keys 1997, p. 3)

The article states that there were no simple answers but that there were several factors to consider including:

- *The use of calculators*
  Nine- and 13-year-olds in England were more likely to use calculators in their maths lessons. The reliance on calculators has been suggested as one possible reason for England's relatively poor standing in maths, but there is no firm evidence to support this view.

- *Classroom organisation*
  In maths the predominant form of teaching for 9-year-olds was to have children working individually with assistance from their teachers. One proposed explanation for England's poor performance in maths was the lack of whole class teaching. However, whole class teaching methods were also infrequently used in science where the approach seemed to be one of having children working in pairs or small groups with assistance from the teacher; and England achieved high scores in science. To complicate the issue whole class teaching methods were more frequently used with 13-year-olds, but the high-achieving countries in maths did not use whole class teaching methods for this age group. The article states that 'it cannot be assumed that more whole class teaching could improve England's mathematics performance' (Keys, 1997, p. 3).

CONCLUDING COMMENTS

The author states that these results are from the first analysis of the data and that what is needed is more detailed investigation to shed light on the factors involved in teaching and learning in these subject areas.

Implications of assessment and categorisation

Possibility of self-fulfilling prophecy

One implication of assessment regards the extent to which feedback on performance affects the expectations an individual has of themselves. Suppose in a primary classroom, let's say Year 1, the class teacher arranges the children into reading groups on the basis of ability and calls each reading group by a different name. There is the green group for the most able students, the yellow group for the average students and the red group for the least able group. The question is when do children begin to make comparisons between their abilities and others'? Do children say: 'I am not clever like so and so, the clever children are in the green group'? Does this realisation of their ability as perceived by the teacher spur them on to try harder or do they internalise their perceived label? If the student internalises the teacher's perceptions, then this would be an example of a self-fulfilling prophecy.

This is a complex issue. Rosenthal and Jacobson (1968) conducted a classic study in this area, focusing on the role of the teacher. Teachers were told on the basis of IQ test results that certain students were identified as late bloomers and that these students would really come on academically. Eight months later IQ tests were given to all students. It was found that the late bloomers had improved their IQ test scores by as much as 30 IQ points, whereas those not indicated as late bloomers showed no significant improvement. The key point in this study is that the students identified as late bloomers were not chosen on the basis of IQ test scores but were in fact chosen randomly from the class register. It would seem that the only difference between the students was the teacher's expectations. (For a full description of this study see Chapter 10.) More recent research into this area has looked at the consequences of setting or streaming for students' self-expectations.

Setting or streaming

One of the consequences of student assessment is to place students in ability groups. OFSTED reports have revealed a growing trend towards ability sets rather than mixed ability groups. One possible reason for this trend could be that teachers feel that ability groups are more suited to the National Curriculum's structured and tiered format (Sukhnandan 1999). However, the question remains as to how grouping students according to ability affects attainment. A review of evidence in this area conducted by the Nfer revealed that:

- Some studies suggest that setting has a positive effect on student ability.
- Some studies suggest that mixed ability groups have a positive effect on student ability.

- Other studies suggest that setting works better than mixed ability teaching for certain subjects such as mathematics, science and modern languages.

Overall there seems to be no conclusive evidence for or against setting. However an analysis of the research reveals that this is a complex issue and other factors need to be taken into account when trying to explain why setting might work for one group or one individual and not for another.

- Teachers with the most experience and qualifications are allocated to teach the top ability groups.
- Teachers prefer to teach the top sets. They have higher expectations and more positive attitudes towards the top sets than they do towards the bottom sets.
- High ability groups benefit from better resources, higher quality of instruction and more experienced teachers.
- If setting is not carefully done, it can apply to all subject areas regardless of individual differences. A pupil might be a high achiever in all subjects except maths, but if placed in the top set for maths the pupil could experience difficulties.
- The competitive atmosphere that typifies the top set can have detrimental effects on girls.
- Regardless of the ability level of the set, the degree to which the teacher can modify the curriculum and their teaching style to suit their students will have an impact on learning.
- Setting has a detrimental effect on the attitudes and self-esteem of pupils of middle and low ability.
- Once categorised, pupils tend to perform according to the set to which they are assigned.
- Low ability pupils placed in low ability sets are denied the support of more able students who can act as positive role models.

(Sukhnandan 1999, Sukhnandan and Lee 1998)

Sukhnandan (1999) suggests that schools need to carefully monitor their systems of pupil organisation so that any negative effects can be identified and addressed.

1 Conduct a short investigation into the style of classroom organisation which your school uses.

2 As part of this investigation you could hand out a short questionnaire to determine students' experiences of classroom organisation. (As in any study ethical guidelines as stipulated by the BPS need to be adhered to.)

Issues of segregation and inclusion

One obvious issue regarding assessment and categorisation is the fact that some students will be deemed to have special educational needs and will need to be placed within special schools. This is a complex issue. On the one hand you have arguments regarding which system, mainstream or special, would offer a student the better education. On the other hand you have arguments regarding issues of human rights. Some theorists would state that separation creates rather than remediates disabilities (Tomlinson 1982, Skirtic 1991). This view sees disability as a social construction. Disability is not a trait that is possessed by the individual but one that is acquired by how society treats an individual. If children are segregated from other children at an early age, what does this communicate to the individual? The Centre for the Study of Inclusive Education affirms that:

> Children would not be devalued or discriminated against by being excluded or sent away because of their disability or learning difficulty. There are no legitimate reasons to separate children for the duration of their schooling. They belong together rather than need to be protected from one another.
>
> (1996, p. 10)

The argument is that segregation leads to a perceived need for segregation.

Summary

In this chapter we have outlined the value of assessment in referral for intervention, diagnosis of specific need, setting or streaming and evaluation of progress. Various psychometric tests and various forms of assessment have been looked at. Central to all forms of educational assessment are the concepts of validity and reliability. All forms of assessment have limitations and advantages; knowledge of these is necessary in interpreting assessment results in order to make informed decisions.

Review exercise

Describe what methods you would use to measure the understanding of concepts outlined in this chapter.

(Hint: use the terminology. Would you use formative or summative methods? Discuss how you would deal with issues of reliability and validity.)

Further reading

Clarke, S. (1998) *Targeting Assessment in the Primary Classroom*, Abingdon: Hodder & Stoughton. A very approachable and practical book which looks at issues of assessment within the classroom.

Sukhnandan, L. and Lee, B. (1998) *Streaming, Setting and Grouping by Ability, a Review of the Literature*, Slough: Nfer. A very comprehensive, easy-to-read review of the literature in this area.

The following journals provide interesting but perhaps complex articles which illustrate current thinking on assessment. Useful for teacher reference.

Assessment in Education

Educational Researcher

Special educational needs

Introduction

This chapter aims to provide an overview of issues surrounding special educational needs. As we shall see, special educational needs is a catch-all phrase that encompasses an incredibly vast range of difficulties and disabilities. On a general level schools will follow the Code of Practice. The Code of Practice is a government document, which offers guidance relating to how students with special educational needs should be assessed. The assessment follows a staged model, with each stage signifying differing levels of monitoring and intervention. Some children with special educational needs will be issued with a **statement** while others will have an IEP, an individual educational plan. While an overview of a number of different types of special needs is given, the causes, effects, intervention strategies and evaluations of these strategies will be considered in relation to the condition of **dyslexia**. In addition this chapter will focus on the issue of gifted children.

Definitions of special educational need

The 1981 Education Act introduced the concept of identifying children with special educational needs. According to the Act:

> A child has special educational needs if he or she has a learning difficulty, which calls for special educational provision to be made for him.
> A child has a learning difficulty if:

- S/he has a significantly greater difficulty in learning than the majority of the children of her/his age; or
- S/he has a disability, which either prevents or hinders her/him from making use of the educational facilities of a kind generally provided in schools within the area of the local authority concerned for children of his age.

(Cited in Daniels *et al.* 1999)

A global approach to assessment

The Code of Practice

The Code of Practice (1994) expands on the issue of special educational need and offers guidance to schools in regard to identifying, assessing, providing for and monitoring such students. The Code recommends the 'general adoption of a staged model of special educational needs' (p. 9) known as key routes or stages.

Staged model or key route system

STAGE 1: SCHOOL-BASED IDENTIFICATION, ASSESSMENT AND ACTION

The process begins when a parent, teacher or other professional expresses a concern in regard to an individual's progress. The concern could be of an academic, social, or emotional nature. In terms of academic progress, concern would be expressed if the child were not attaining the age-appropriate levels as outlined within the key stages of the National Curriculum. At this stage all relevant parties including the headteacher and parents are informed. The issue of concern is investigated and the child's name is placed on the Special Needs register. From the teacher's perspective this means that they need to keep a special watch on that individual's progress. A child may stay on stage 1 for a few months then come off, or a child may proceed to stage 2.

STAGE 2: ADVICE FROM SUPPORT SERVICES

Once a child's name is placed on the Special Needs register the school's special educational needs co-ordinator (SENCO) will take responsibility for making provision for that child alongside the child's teacher. A key element in this provision is the production, implementation and review of individual educational plans (IEPs). Advice may be sought from other professionals.

STAGE 3: DIRECT INVOLVEMENT FROM SUPPORT AGENCIES

If there is continuing concern regarding whether current provision is meeting the child's needs, at this stage the teachers and SENCO will call for additional support advice and involvement from other professionals including an educational psychologist.

STAGE 4: STATUTORY (FORMAL) ASSESSMENT

The local education authority, LEA, on advice from the educational psychologist, will decide if a statutory assessment of the child is needed. The parents will be informed of this decision. The LEA will need to gather information about the child's special needs from the following sources: parents, school reports, educational psychologists' and medical reports. Once the relevant information is collected the LEA will then make a decision with regard to whether they will proceed to making a statement of special educational needs.

STAGE 5: STATEMENT OF SPECIAL EDUCATIONAL NEEDS

The parents can normally expect a decision on whether the LEA will proceed to making a statement within twelve weeks from commencement of assessment. A statement is a legal document issued by the LEA in circumstances where it has been found upon investigation that an individual has special educational needs which cannot reasonably be provided for within the normal resources available to a particular school. Resources are defined to include funding, staff time and special equipment. When the LEA has issued a statement the LEA has a legal obligation to provide the resources as mentioned in the statement.

Who has special needs?

As of January 1999 approximately 250,000 pupils in schools in England had special educational need (SEN) statements. Sixty per cent of students with statements were educated within mainstream schools (ONS 2000).

In 1998/1999, two out of three pupils in special schools were boys (The Standards Site 2000).

In 1997/1998 the exclusion rate for students with SEN statements was seven times the rate for students without statements (ONS 2000).

Daniels *et al.* (1996) in studying twenty junior schools in one inner city LEA found 'worrying imbalances' in gender and racial backgrounds in regard to certain categories of SEN. The researchers found that male and female black students were more likely to be allocated to the learning difficulty group rather than the reading difficulty group; whereas similar numbers of white students were allocated to the learning difficulty group and the reading difficulty group. Further researchers noted that black males were more likely to be categorised as having emotional and behavioural difficulties than white males. It is stated that further research is needed to determine to what extent teacher assumptions regarding 'black and white masculinity and femininity account for these gender differences' (Arnot *et al.* 1998, p. 65).

Overview of some specific types of learning disabilities

In the previous chapter we looked at how tests such as Wechsler scales were used to assess global learning disabilities. In addition to global learning disabilities an individual could receive a diagnosis of a specific learning disability – for example, dyslexia or a condition such as autism or **Attention Deficit Hyperactivity Disorder (ADHD)**.

Individuals would receive a diagnosis from a combination of doctors, psychologists (educational or clinical) and psychiatrists. Medical reports and diagnostic tools such as the *Diagnostic and Statistical Manual of Mental Disorders*, DSM-IV, and *International Standard Classification of Diseases and Related Health Problems*, ICD-10, would be used. It is crucial to note that many conditions are in fact syndromes. A syndrome is a group of related symptoms or behavioural traits. This means that even individuals with the same condition will not have identical symptoms or behavioural traits. To complicate this situation, one individual will often have more than one type of disability. Professionals refer to this as **co-morbidity**. For example, one student might have dyslexia with ADHD. To complicate the issue further there might be additional physical or sensory disabilities, medical conditions, such as epilepsy, or mental health issues, such as depression. The reality is that this complexity in diagnosis means that intervention strategies need to be targeted to the individual's unique pattern of strengths and weaknesses. It is also crucial when talking about individuals with learning disabilities or special educational needs that we realise that an individual is first and foremost an individual in their own right and that their own unique personality will be apparent. (See Table 4.1.)

Strategies for educating children with special needs

IEPs

A key element in stage 2 of the Code of Practice is the development of individual educational plans or IEPs. An IEP is appropriate for all students with special educational needs and as such IEPs should be considered as a key intervention. There has been much guidance and commentary in regard to what constitutes an effective IEP. Ramjhun (1995) discusses the features of a good IEP. An IEP will identify the child's current level of attainments. The IEP will then set targets. The targets must be related to the areas of difficulty, and be specific, measurable, achievable and teachable given current resources.

Targets need to be related specifically to success criteria or indicators, which can be objectively measured. The nature of resources or provision needs to be set out and methods of monitoring specified. Monitoring methods include: record keeping, arranging various

Table 4.1 Examples of conditions that will affect learning

Learning disability   Assessment

Learning disability	Assessment
Autism	Today two classification systems are used in the diagnosis of autism: the DSM-IV and ICD-10. The essential criteria from both classification systems are: • Qualitative impairment in reciprocal social interaction. • Qualitative impairment in verbal and non-verbal communication and in imaginative activity. • Markedly restricted repertoire of activities and interests.
Asperger syndrome	The DSM-IV lists the following criteria for Asperger syndrome as: • A lack of any clinically significant delay in language or cognitive development. • Qualitative impairments in reciprocal social interaction. • Restricted, repetitive, and stereotypical pattern of interests and activities.
Down's syndrome	Down's syndrome is the result of a chromosomal anomaly, whereby instead of there being 46 chromosomes in each cell, there are 47. The extra chromosome is a partial or an extra chromosome 21; thus sometimes Down syndrome is referred to as Trisomy 21.
ADHD	The DSM-IV distinguishes between: • Attention Deficit Hyperactivity Disorder Predominantly Inattentive Type. • Attention Deficit Hyperactivity Disorder Predominantly Hyperactive-Impulsive Type. • Attention Deficit Hyperactivity Disorder Combined Type. To receive such a diagnosis the individual will need to have exhibited certain behaviours for at least six months and to a degree that is maladaptive and inconsistent with development levels. An example of *inattention* would be that the individual fails to give close attention to detail or makes careless mistakes in schoolwork or other activities and often has difficulty sustaining attention in tasks or play activities. An example of *hyperactivity* would be that the individual often fidgets with hands or feet or squirms in their seat and often leaves their seat in the classroom or in other situations in which remaining seated is expected. An example of *impulsivity* would be that an individual often blurts out answers before questions have been completed and often has difficulty waiting their turn.

meetings to co-ordinate the provision of IEPs, and of course reviews of IEPs.

IEPs can be very lengthy and complex depending on the individual needs of the student; therefore an example of what an IEP involves will help clarify issues. It must be noted that the example set out in Table 4.2 is very much a simplified version.

Evaluation of IEPs

First we can say that the targets need to be achievable so that the child feels that they are progressing, which in turn would be reinforcing or motivating. However an IEP is an incredibly time-consuming process, especially when you consider that IEPs will need to be constantly monitored and reviewed. Yet constant monitoring is essential in order to determine the extent of progress and continuing need. Dyson (1996), after carrying out research with SENCOs in the former Cleveland LEA, commented that schools might consider a value added criterion when it comes to deciding whether to draw up an IEP; that is, to only consider doing so if the educational benefit to the child could not be secured in a less time- and resource-intensive way.

Picture Exchange Communication System (PECS)

Andrew Bondy and Lori Frost developed the **Picture Exchange Communication System** in the early 1990s when they were working with the Delaware Autistic Program. Although originally the programme was used to foster communication with young autistic children, it is now used with older children and adults who have a range of communication difficulties. The aim of PECS is to give a means of communication to individuals who previously have had none. The system revolves around the concept of exchanging pictures for desired objects. To begin with, the teacher needs to establish what the child finds rewarding. Several objects (crisps, a carton of juice, and various toys) are placed on a table and the child is observed in order to determine what his or her preferences are. Once preferences are established, pictures of preferred objects are made into cards. The next stage of the programme involves the child being shown the picture of the preferred object and the preferred object itself. To receive the preferred object the child must give the picture card to the trainer. Once the child

Table 4.2 Individual educational plan

Name: John Blue   **Age**: 9

Strengths and weaknesses   **Priority**: Attention span

Strengths   **Weaknesses**
John can: John cannot:
- Concentrate for a maximum of   - Keep to a task without almost
  two minutes on a task.   continuous encouragement and
- Co-operate with the teacher and   prompting.
  other children.

Teaching objectives derived from the above:

Objectives   **Strategy**
- Increase his attention on task by   - Participate in a group with two
  thirty seconds per week.   other children learning and
                                                  practising listening and attention
                                                  skills. Sessions will last fifteen
                                                  minutes per day. The Special
                                                  Needs Assistant will run this group
                                                  five days a week.
                                                - The Special Needs Assistant will
                                                  create a star chart with John
                                                  recording his attention on specific
                                                  tasks. If his attention on tasks
                                                  increases by one minute per week
                                                  he will be allowed extra time on
                                                  the computer which he enjoys.

Success criteria   **Contingency arrangement**
- By the end of the school year to   - Review progress in regard to
  have increased his attention on   attention span. If John has not
  task to fifteen minutes.   increased his attention span by
                                                  one minute after a month, then
                                                  John will participate in two
                                                  fifteen-minute sessions per day in
                                                  regard to attention skills.

Provision	Monitoring assessment
Material and resources: • School-designed booklet for Attention Skills Group. Staffing: • Special Needs Assistant's time • Class teacher's time	• Daily written records. • Weekly planning review meetings with Special Needs Assistant, teacher and SENCO as required. • Written communication with mother via home book once a week. • Meeting with parents once a term.

has done this, they receive the preferred object. To begin with, the child might need some physical guidance and prompting. This is the first exchange. From these small beginnings other picture cards are introduced. Eventually children are encouraged to use picture cards in combination to form sentences. Children using this system will carry around personalised books of picture cards, which include a Velcro strip to which they add picture cards (backed with Velcro) to form sentences.

Bondy and Frost (1994) summarising work with eighty-five autistic pre-school children over five years found that:

- Almost all children learned to use one picture to communicate a request within one month of starting the programme.
- 95 per cent of children learned to use two or more pictures.
- 76 per cent of the children developed some speech through the training programme.

In summary, the programme not only offered a practical form of communication to those who had none but, for many, speech developed with the use of this programme.

Social skills training

Many individuals with global learning disabilities and individuals with autism or Asperger syndrome will benefit from social skills training.

This issue becomes increasingly important as the individual prepares to leave school and enter the adult world of work and further training. Social skills programmes would cover such areas as greetings, appropriate eye contact, welcoming visitors, accepting correction, speaking with authority figures and conversation skills. Most programmes cover the following components. The individual by themselves or in a group will receive specific instructions in regard to a specific skill. The teacher will demonstrate the social skill. Next there will be role play where the individual practises the skill. Then there will be feedback, possibly more role play and rehearsal. Howlin and Yates (1996) reported the following benefits after a social skills programme aimed at adults with autism:

- Speech became less repetitive.
- Improvement in conversational skills including offering information and asking questions.

However, Howlin and Yates (1996) note that there are problems in generalising skills acquired in the group setting of a social skills class to the outside world. Howlin (1997) tells the story of Jerome, who within the context of a social skills group received instruction on how to initiate and maintain conversations with young women. Even with training Jerome found it difficult to meet women, until he came up with a solution.

> His solution for finding the best place to meet as many single women as possible was a simple one – inside the local ladies lavatory! When arrested by the police, he clearly had no perception of why this behaviour had got him into trouble.
>
> (Howlin 1997, p. 92)

Another way of improving complex social skills involves the creation of social stories. An example of a social story is given in Chapter 10.

A friend tells you of her recent visit to her child's school. She tells you that she was informed that her 7-year-old son is being placed on the Special Needs Register at stage 1 as outlined by the Code of Practice. If her son progresses to stage 2 then the SENCO and the classroom teacher will produce an IEP. Your friend is confused by the terminology.

Explain the process to her.

Progress exercise 4.1

Dyslexia

Causes

Dyslexia has been defined as: 'a disorder manifested by difficulty in learning to read, despite conventional instruction, adequate intelligence and socio-cultural opportunity' (Critchley 1970, p. 11).

In terms of a cause it was first speculated that dyslexia could be attributed to deficits in the visual system as certain children with dyslexia were prone to reversing letters, such as reading a '*b*' for a '*d*'. However, more recent research (Shaywitz 1996) has argued that dyslexia should be seen as a deficit in language processing involving, in particular, problems with phonological decoding. **Phonemes** are the distinctive linguistic or sound units that in combination create words. Knowledge of the association between verbal sounds and the corresponding written form is a skill necessary for reading and writing. For example, the word cat is made up of three sounds, *kuh – aah – tuh*, but is spelt cat. There are twenty-six letters in the alphabet and these letters in combination form the forty-four sounds that the English language employs. The difficulty in reading and spelling is that words are often not spelt the way they sound and that different letter combinations represent the same sound. For example, Hardwick (1997) states that the ee sound can be spelt in ten different ways. They are: e (me), ee (see), ey (key), ea (eat), ie (thief), ei (seize), e-e (cede), eo (people), i-e (magazine) and ae (encyclopaedia).

Ellis (1993) postulated a simple model for reading which can be applied to individuals with dyslexia. Ellis's model utilises the following components:

- *Visual Analysis System*: recognition of shapes and position of shapes.
- *Visual Input Lexicon*: word-by-word recognition or internal dictionary for word form.
- *Semantic System*: recognition of word meaning.
- *Speech Output Lexicon*: sound recognition for whole word.
- *Phoneme Level*: knowledge of distinctive speech sounds that comprise words.
- *Speech*: ability to produce speech.

What Ellis (1993) is proposing is that all of these components are necessary to the reading process. If there is difficulty in one of the components it does not imply that reading is impossible but that it becomes more difficult as alternative or less optimal pathways need to be taken. This view could be used to explain the difficulties faced by dyslexic individuals. This view would also imply that there could be several reasons why an individual was having difficulty with reading.

In order to understand dyslexia, consideration of the stages of normal reading development is needed. At the earliest stage, words are identified on the basis of visual appearance. The child is making no use of letter–sound correspondence and will make mistakes such as confusing *black* for *back*, as both words are of similar length and start and end with the same letters. Children then progress on to the second stage of reading which involves the use of phonics.

Just to complicate the issue it is worth noting that controversy exists as to whether there is such a condition as dyslexia. Dyslexia is diagnosed due to the discrepancy between overall intelligence or ability and specific scores on reading and spelling tests. This view implies that students who are good at most tasks but not reading and spelling will receive a diagnosis of dyslexia, but those students who are poor at all tasks will not be considered dyslexic even though they might have the same problems. However, Aaron *et al.* (1988) argue that the cause of developmental dyslexia is poor grapheme–phoneme (letter–sound) decoding skills, whereas the cause of general reading delay with overall low levels of ability is poor comprehension. On a practical level, what is important is that, if a child is having difficulty with reading or spelling, intervention is given.

Effects of dyslexia

In some ways the effects of dyslexia are stated within the definition as an inability to read and write. Certainly ours is a literate society, with the consequence that an inability to read and write would put an individual at a great disadvantage. Magazines, books and information on computers are all presented in a written format. We need to read to fill in forms: forms to enrol for courses; forms to open a bank account; forms to apply for a job, a driving licence, a passport – the list is endless. In addition to difficulties with reading and spelling, some individuals with dyslexia will experience difficulties in regard to maths, remembering, following complex instructions, telling right from left and attending to tasks. Though the effects are in some ways apparent there can be additional effects.

- Reading and spelling are basic prerequisite skills needed in order to progress through the key stages of the National Curriculum.
- A competence at reading and spelling is needed if the child is to achieve their academic potential.
- If diagnosis is not made, secondary negative effects could occur. Teachers might label the child as lazy. The child, in trying to make sense of their inability to succeed at a task that their peers are mastering, might label himself or herself as stupid. This in turn could lead to lower levels of self-esteem and possibly to disruptive behaviour.

It has been argued that diagnosis needs to be made as early as possible so as to prevent the child from experiencing failure.

Specific strategies for educating children with dyslexia

In relation to dyslexia there are a number of educational interventions. These include structured written language programmes and multi-sensory teaching. Structured language programmes include the 'Alpha to Omega Programme' and the 'Bangor Teaching Programme'. A structured programme sees learning to read and spell as the acquisition of skills. The skills are cumulative in that basic skills need to be laid down before more complex skills can be taught. In terms of a written language programme the sequence of skill acquisition would be as follows: letters, sound/symbol correspondence, blends (combinations of sounds), regular words, polysyllabic words and syllabic division. The teacher would need to assess what skills the child has and start from there.

Multi-sensory techniques involve the teaching of phonics, but with an approach that uses the inter-relation between sensory modalities, i.e. the connections between auditory, visual, kinaesthetic and tactile modalities. Let us take the word cat. The individual hears the word *cat* (auditory), sees the word *cat* (visual), says the word *cat* (auditory), prints the word *cat* (kinaesthetic) and feels the word *cat* (tactile as it is written in wooden two-dimensional letters). The rationale is that if there is a weakness with one modality then there is a need to find an alternative way of learning which capitalises on existing strengths in other modalities (Thomson 1990).

'Teaching Today' (*Dyslexia in the Primary Classroom* 1997) gives the following examples of multi-sensory teaching:

- Have children look in a mirror when reading words so that they can see how sounds are formed by lip and tongue movements. This task is useful for auditory discrimination, such as distinguishing the sound *f* from *th*.
- Tracing the letter shape on the table, in sand, in the air or on someone's back helps to establish what arm and hand movements correspond to what letter. This process is enhanced if the child does the movement with a blindfold on.
- With eyes shut the child holds a wooden letter to feel and identify the letter.
- Running around big shapes and letters in the playground establishes a whole-body feel for the shapes involved.

Further ideas are suggested by Hardwick (1997) and include:

- Having students make their own tapes of spelling words to learn. For instance, the child presses the button on the tape machine and first hears themselves saying *eat*, then the child pauses the tape machine, writes the word *eat*, pushes the play button again and hears themselves spelling *eat*. They then pause the tape machine and check their spelling. This process can be repeated.
- Flashcards can be used. On one side of the flashcard write the target word, for example, *my*. On the other side of the flashcard have the

child write a sentence with the word *my* in it, that is, something personally meaningful to them – for example, 'My favourite animal is a hedgehog.' Then have the child draw a picture, perhaps of a hedgehog. It is hoped that the personally meaningful sentence and the visual picture will serve as a reminder of what the word looks like (Hardwick 1996).

Evaluation

Research, to date, has served to identify which factors lead to successful teaching for dyslexic children – see Table 4.3.

What is still not known is what teaching method is suitable for a particular child with dyslexia. Dyslexic children, though sharing common difficulties with reading and spelling, will have their unique

Table 4.3 Factors relating to teaching students with dyslexia

Students with dyslexia do improve with:	*Students with dyslexia do not improve with:*
• Multi-sensory techniques. • Individualised instruction based on careful assessment. • Small-group or one-to-one teaching. • Early identification. • Understanding and encouragement. • A structured approach based on phonetic principles. • Teaching to strengths and offering remedial teaching aimed at weakness where appropriate. • Mnemonics • Help with organisational skills. • Exciting classroom experiences and constructive support.	• Unspecific methods, i.e. more reading or spelling. • More attention. • Being left to grow out of it. • Training in visual or auditory skills alone (unless focused on written language). • Patterning or other neurological exercises to develop laterality. • Punishments or threats. • Inappropriate labelling.

Source: Adapted from Thomson 1990, p. 213.

cognitive profiles outlining weakness and strengths. The question remains as to whether to teach to strengths only or whether to try to compensate for weakness. In terms of Ellis's theoretical model of reading, if the phoneme level is damaged, will intensive teaching time result in improved phonological awareness, or should teaching time be used to teach reading via a method that capitalises on strengths? This issue was raised in an interesting case study (Brooks 1995) where an 11-year-old boy with severe specific learning difficulties/dyslexia was systematically tested after a variety of intervention programmes aimed to improve spelling. The boy, referred to as RG in the case study, was assessed as having a reading age of 7 years and 6 months and a spelling age of 7 years and 5 months. Further tests revealed that RG had weaknesses in phonological skills and auditory memory. To assess various teaching interventions, sets of words of similar difficulty were taught by different teaching strategies and the success of each teaching strategy was measured by words learned. The teaching strategies included:

- *Look and say*: the teacher says the word and shows the word on a card for ten seconds.
- *Tracing*: the student is shown the word and asked to *say the word* and *trace the letters of the word* as if writing them (Fernald 1943).
- *Simultaneous oral spelling*: the teacher writes the word. The student is asked to *write the word*, copying from the teacher's writing and at the same time *naming each letter of the word* as the student writes the word. The student is then asked to *name the word* and to check that the word has been written correctly by comparing it with the teacher's version (Bryant and Bradley 1985).
- *Words in words*: the student is shown the word on a card and the teacher draws attention to any meaningful parts of the word. For example, *damaged* contains *dam* and *age*.
- *Phonics*: the student is shown the word. The teacher sounds out the word. The sound corresponding to each phoneme is represented by a letter. The teacher repeats the word. The student is asked to sound out the word as the teacher has done and then to say the word. For example, *c-ar-t* makes *cart*.
- *Rules*: the teacher shows the word on a card and indicates any rules from the Cowdery Scheme. For example, it is appropriate to spell *skittles* with *sk* rather than *sc* as the rule states that *sk* is followed by the vowels, *e*, *i*, or *y* (Cowdery *et al*. 1983).

- *Baseline*: word cards are shown to the student. The student is required to say the word then spell the word without the card being present. The student receives no instruction and is not told whether they are correct or not.

It was found that some methods produced better results than others did. For RG the Look and say, Tracing, Words in words and Rule conditions produced significant improvements in spelling over the Baseline, Phonics and Simultaneous oral spelling conditions. The method of Words in words produced the maximum amount of words learned. It would seem that the method of Words in words, instead of focusing on what the student found difficult – that is, being aware of phonemes – capitalised on his strengths. Brooks, commenting on this case study, states that the results have implications for how individuals with dyslexia are taught. The use of a structured approach to teaching, re-inforcement and monitoring was not sufficient alone to produce significant improvements. To ensure effective learning an investigation was needed to determine what method worked best.

Dyslexia is a condition that affects many adults and children within this country. There is currently more awareness of the condition and current research is being geared to early diagnosis and intervention and to establishing what types of intervention work best for what individuals.

Gifted children

There have been many definitions of gifted. Robinson (1981) distinguishes between the 'garden variety gifted', children with high IQs in the range of 130–150 but without any extraordinary ability in any one given area, and 'highly gifted' children, children with high IQs and extraordinary abilities in one or more areas. The National Association for Gifted Children (2000, p. 1) offers the following definitions:

- '*Openly able*: enjoying their talent and excelling in all they do.'
- '*Concealed able*: under-achievers who fade into and hide in their peer-group.'
- '*Rebellious able*: disruptive under-achievers with a range of behavioural problems.'

- '*Creative able*: "odd-balls" often with unusual divergent thought patterns, which can make them intense and abrasive.'
- '*Talented able*: intellectually able but with a particular talent in one area.'

The National Association for Gifted Children (2000) finds this framework useful in that it points out the difficulty in diagnosis. They argue that a teacher would easily be able to pick up the openly able and talented able, but miss the concealed able and creative able, and label the rebellious able as just disruptive. Returning to the issue of assessment, the National Association for Gifted Children (2000) state that the following sources are used for the identification of gifted children:

- Teacher observations (checklists)
- Parental observations
- Peer-group nomination
- Evidence from pupil's work
- Pupil's own interests
- Tests (cognitive ability tests)
- National Curriculum tests
- Evidence from out-of-school activities

Assuming that teachers have identified the gifted children, what next? The government suggests a wider range of strategies for grouping pupils, including setting by subject ability, acceleration (placing child in older class), fast-tracking, withdrawing the gifted student for additional adult support, master-classes, summer schools, mentoring and work experience (DfEE 1999, 'Every school should have a clear policy for gifted children'; DfEE 2000a, *National Literacy and Numeracy Strategies: Guidance on Teaching Able Children*).

Teachers are also required to rethink how they will plan their lessons, what specific strategies they will use for more able students, the type of questioning they will use with the child and the use of extension material. In terms of the Numeracy hour the following suggestions are made:

- Direct questions to able pupils.
- Include more open questioning to allow all pupils to respond at their own level to the same question.

- Encourage pupils to explore alternative mental strategies.
- Reduce whole class activity, setting stepped tasks, encouraging able pupils to omit earlier steps.
- Reduce amount of time able pupils spend on practice and consolidation.
- Target teaching in ability groups.
- Use a range of open tasks/investigations that all pupils can access at their own level.
- Encourage sustained work that able pupils may continue over two or more lessons.

(DfEE 2000a)

Summary

In this chapter we have seen that the term special educational needs covers an incredible array of difficulties and disabilities, including dyslexia, autism, ADHD and Down syndrome. In terms of assessment, the Code of Practice outlines a staged model, requiring differing levels of monitoring and intervention. Monitoring often takes the form of writing IEPs and setting targets. In some cases individual students will require statements. Dyslexia was discussed in terms of causes, effects, suggested interventions and evaluations of intervention strategies. Dyslexia, like many learning disabilities, is a syndrome, or a group of related symptoms or behavioural traits. As such, individuals with dyslexia, though experiencing common difficulties, will have unique patterns of strengths and weaknesses. Any intervention strategy would need to take this fact into account. The issue of gifted children was discussed. Recent initiatives have recognised that, while most schools have many policies in place to help their least able students, the most able students are often neglected. To remedy the situation certain strategies are currently being formulated. Research into special educational needs in regard to assessment, intervention strategies and evaluation of such strategies is ongoing.

Imagine that you are a teacher and you are asked to write a brief document outlining the school's policy in regard to special educational needs. This document will be for the use of parents and as such needs to be informative and reader-friendly.

Further reading

Thomson, M. (1990) *Developmental Dyslexia*, 3rd edn, London: Whurr Publishers. A very informative and detailed book. Recommended as a reference tool.

Journals such as *Special Children* give a real flavour of what is happening within today's classroom.

For further information contact:

Dyslexia Institute, 133 Gresham Road, Staines, Middlesex TW18 2AJ. Internet address: http://www.dyslexia-Inst.org.uk/

Cultural and gender diversity

Introduction

There have been many headlines in the papers regarding differences in educational performance on the basis of culture and gender. Recently there has been much made of the success of girls in achieving more of the top grades in GCSE and A level exams. This trend emerged in the 1990s. This chapter aims to get behind the headlines and look at the facts in order to explain which girls and which boys achieve. Specifically this chapter will examine what factors account for achievement and underachievement and what strategies have been developed to tackle underachievement. We will see that this is a very complex issue.

Differences in educational performance

One of the advantages of national assessment is that it is possible through an analysis of results to talk about differential performance, or what group does better at what subject under what circumstances. Of course it is important to remember that when we are looking at statistical results concerning large groups we are looking at overall trends, and that these trends will obscure both the results of subgroups and individual differences. But what are the facts?

Gender

Key stages

From an analysis of the 1995 SAT results the following facts are established (Arnot *et al.* 1998):

- Girls get off to a better start in reading at Key Stage 1 and this advantage is maintained throughout Key Stages 2 and 3 and evident in GCSE results. These results reflect results in other countries and it would seem that girls' superiority in language is a world-wide phenomenon.
- Boys and girls perform similarly in maths at all key stages.
- After making comparable starts in science, boys begin to pull ahead of girls at Key Stage 2.

In summarising the above results, Arnot *et al.* (1998, p. 8) claim that: 'blanket statements about girls performing better than boys or vice versa are difficult to justify; reference should always be made to a specific aspect of the curriculum.' Furthermore there is an equal number of boys and girls at all attainment levels and 20 per cent of boys and girls get off to a bad start.

Table 5.1 **Performance in key stages by gender (1995)**

% of students achieving level	English % boys	English % girls	Maths % boys	Maths % girls	Science % boys	Science % girls
Age 7 Level 2+	73	83	77	81	83	86
Age 11 Level 4+	42	56	44	45	71	68
Age 14 Level 6+	14	26	34	33	27	23
Age 16 GCSE (A*–C)	48.8	65.7	45.5	44.3	47	48

Source: Adapted from Arnot *et al.* 1998, pp. 5–10.

Progress exercise 5.1

1 At each key stage state whether boys or girls are performing better at English, science or maths

2 Check recent results. Are there any new trends?

GCSE

In GCSE there has been a clear trend (Arnot *et al.* 1999). A twenty-year analysis reveals the following:

- From 1975 to 1987 an equal number of boys and girls were achieving five or more A–C passes, that is, for every 100 girls attaining this level, there were between 94 and 100 boys.
- From 1987 to 1990 there was a period of rapid change during which girls started to outperform boys in achieving the higher grades at GCSE.
- From 1990 to 1995 a new period of stability and inequality emerged, that is, for every 100 girls achieving this level of attainment, there were between 80 and 83 boys.
- The percentage of pupils achieving five or more A*–C grades at GCSE in 1995, according to gender, was 48 per cent for girls and 39 per cent for boys.
- In 1999, 10 per cent more girls than boys achieved five or more A*–C grades at GCSE (Standards Site 2000).

A level

We can now look at the relationship between gender and A level results. In the 1970s, although girls attained high grades at the age of 16, most did not achieve three good A level results, thus they were denied the opportunity of proceeding to higher education. This was seen as an indication of female underachievement (Arnot *et al*. 1999). 'In 1987/88 an equal proportion of young men and women achieved two or more A levels or equivalent but since 1988/1989 women have outperformed men at this level' (ONS 2000, p. 58).

Evaluation

In summary, what can be seen from these statistics is that there has been a shift in terms of achievement, with girls taking the lead. However, the facts mentioned so far rather than closing the debate on differences in educational performance raise many questions. Arnot *et al*. (1999) pose the following questions:

- What factors can account for males' recent lack of success in GCSE examinations?
- How are the differential educational performances seen in a discussion of gender affected by other social and educational factors such as social class, ethnic background and locality of school?

Arnot *et al.* (1999) further commented on the fact that, despite girls' increased educational and academic achievement, women still experience discrimination and disadvantages in the workplace.

Other factors

Types of schools

The type of school attended has also been said to have an effect on academic achievement, as Table 5.2 illustrates.

Table 5.2 Percentage of 15+-year old pupils achieving five or more A*–C grades at GCSE according to type of school (1995)

School type	% of boys achieving 5+ A*–C grades	% of girls achieving 5+ A*–C grades
Girls' comprehensive		46%
Boys' comprehensive	36%	
Mixed comprehensive	35%	44%
Selective	93%	95%
Modern	22%	30%

Source: Adapted from OFSTED analysis 1996, as cited in Arnot *et al.* 1998, p. 44.

1 To what extent do girls achieve more than boys in single sex, mixed sex, and selective schools?

2 To what extent are boys' and girls' achievement levels affected by type of schooling?

3 What can we conclude from these data?

Progress exercise 5.2

Social class, ethnic origin and gender

To give a feel of the complexity in determining which girls and which boys do well, Table 5.3 looks at GCSE results (1985) according to social class, ethnic origin and gender.

Table 5.3 Average GCSE examination scores by social class, ethnic origin and gender (1985)

Ethnic origin and social class	Number of individuals studied	Average male exam score	Average female exam score
Asian			
Professional	17	30.7	27.8
Intermediate	95	27.2	25.9
Manual	189	23.3	22.5
African Caribbean			
Professional	12	27.1	24.9
Intermediate	68	21.1	18.1
Manual	115	14.3	15.6
White			
Professional	2,118	30.4	32.3
Intermediate	3,093	23.7	25.6
Manual	5,218	17.6	20.6

Source: Adapted from Gillborn and Gipps 1996, p. 16.

Progress exercise 5.3

1 Which group has the highest and the lowest exam score?

2 Do girls always outperform boys?

Analysis of the 1998 GCSE results (ONS 2000) reveals that in all ethnic groups girls do as well as or outperform boys. The greatest difference in boy/girl performance was for students from the black group: 42 per cent of black girls achieved one to four GCSE passes at grades A* to C, compared to 24 per cent of black boys. A greater proportion of Indian boys and girls achieved higher grades at GCSE than any other ethnic group. This trend continued at A levels, with 36 per cent of Indian pupils achieving two or more A levels. Only 29 per cent of white students achieved this standard.

The document, *Recent Research on the Achievements of Ethnic Minority Pupils* (Gillborn and Gipps 1996), reaches the following conclusions:

- 'Whatever the pupil's gender or ethnic origin those from higher social class backgrounds do better on average' (p. 17).
- 'Black over-representation in exclusions is a widespread problem, affecting both primary and secondary schools. . . . The figure for Black Caribbean young people is the worst, almost six times the rate of exclusion for whites' (p. 52).

However, pupils from nearly all ethnic minorities are more likely to continue with further or higher education than their white counterparts. In 1998 students from ethnic minorities accounted for 13 per cent of higher education students (under the age of 20) in the UK. Students from ethnic minorities are said to be over-represented in higher education as only 9 per cent of the population under the age of 20 are enrolled in higher education classes. However, students from Indian and Chinese groups are more likely to enter higher education than those from other ethnic groups. Young black Caribbean men and young Bangladeshi and Pakistani women are under-represented in higher education (ONS 2000).

Explanations for differential performance

As we have seen in the first part of this chapter, many factors, such as gender, social class, ethnic origin and type of schooling, and an interaction of these factors, contribute to differing levels of educational attainment. How do we explain the differential performances? It would seem that perhaps different explanations are required for different groups. We are not only interested in why students underachieve but also in what factors contribute to exceptional achievement.

Why have girls succeeded?

Biological explanations

Are girls just naturally better at English, whereas boys are naturally better at science? Arnot *et al.* (1998) argue that the biological determination model cannot account for educational achievement differences in terms of gender as it has been found that sex differences vary across cultures, across time within the same culture and also through the life of individuals. If biology cannot account for the differences, should we look perhaps at differing cultural expectations?

New attitudes

In the 1950s women were encouraged to stay at home and raise children rather than pursue a career. However, certainly by the 1990s attitudes had changed. Girls were talking of gender equality and valuing individual achievement. It is clear from the facts mentioned earlier in this chapter that girls have been achieving more in terms of qualifications. However Chisholm and du Bois-Reymond (1993) noted that a significant proportion still hold on to traditional values regarding marriage and that for many their academic achievements are used to signify their intellectual credentials, rather than being used to move out of their class. Arnot *et al.* (1999) argue that more and more women see educational achievements as necessary in today's world. In generations past, many women have relied on their husbands to support them. But now?

> Young women were increasingly reluctant to commit themselves to marriage, seeing it as but one option out of many forms of partnership. Different models for linking childbearing with employment became a viable choice, as were alternative life styles and sexualities. In this context, educational qualifications would not only be an investment, they would be an essential part of self-protection and survival in an increasingly insecure world.
>
> (Arnot *et al.* 1999, pp. 123–124)

The value of single sex education

There has been a lot written in the media concerning the value of single sex schools. It would seem reasonable to suppose that single sex schools would allow both boys and girls to concentrate on the required work rather than on the dynamics of interacting with each other. However, it would appear from the facts mentioned earlier that this is not the case. Arnot *et al.* (1998) conclude that the 'apparently superior performance of single sex (and especially girls-only) institutions has been largely due to the initially superior performance of the pupils entering these schools' (p. 46). This would suggest that single sex institutions cannot explain the improvement in girls' performance over recent years.

Why do girls do better at English?

Arnot *et al.* (1998) argue that the differences in educational achievement in regard to English are a consequence of how both boys and girls see the studying of English in relation to how they define themselves as male or female.

'Boys perceive the literacy experience as female because, from an early age, reading and writing are associated with feminine forms of expression, especially the exploration of personal experience and feelings in stories and poetry' (Arnot *et al.* 1998, p. 29). Perhaps boys would not want to excel at a subject that they have labelled feminine. Perhaps girls' superior performance in English can be attributed to the manner in which English is taught and to the fact that English is perceived as a feminine subject. However, it has been found that boys express a preference for reading non-fiction. While their reading preferences might not help them in an analysis of the metaphors used in *Hamlet*, their reading preferences might contribute more to a successful career than a good GCSE grade (White 1986, Alloway and Gilbert 1997). As a way forward it has been suggested that the 'value of reading and writing non-fiction, and combining physical and verbal activity in the study and acting of plays, may be insufficiently acknowledged and developed in the curriculum. This may disadvantage boys and possibly girls' (Arnot *et al.* 1998, p. 29).

Why do some students from lower social classes and minority ethnic groups underachieve?

Here we get into an argument, which tries to mesh the factors of gender, lower social class, race and educational achievement. A lot has been written about the 'macho lads'. Indeed this 'new laddish', 'anti-school', 'behaving badly' attitude has been identified as the consequence of economic decline and one of the main reasons for male under-achievement. This argument (Arnot *et al.* 1999) centres on how the structure of paid employment has changed dramatically within the last few decades, with males in lower socio-economic classes having taken the brunt of these changes. The last few decades have seen the contraction of manufacturing and the labour market and the replacement of factory work with an emphasis on new technology. The new careers are in areas such as computing and biogenetics. Such fields call for well-qualified, highly skilled and highly educated individuals. While years ago a young male with minimal educational qualifications could leave school and find a job, those days have gone. Many young men have experienced their fathers losing jobs and in turn have reduced expectations of finding work. The question now revolves around how a male forms a masculine identity in the face of unemployment. In addition to changes in the job market, schools, in response to the National Curriculum and publicised league tables, have become more competitive places. Setting and streaming have become more popular within schools, with the consequence that the lower sets have proportionately more boys and more pupils from ethnic minorities. One could argue that boys need not be in the lower sets if only they set their minds to it and worked. Here we get into the relationship between peer group culture and the value it puts on academic success. Can males from lower working-class backgrounds really work hard, achieve those grades and still be seen as one of the lads? Is working hard at school seen as girls' stuff? By working hard will they be seen as a traitor to their class? Do such attitudes exist? Mac an Ghaill (1994) studied a group of working-class boys and found that the macho lads responded to academic failure and their poor employment prospects by 'celebrating the 3 Fs – fighting, football and fucking'. These lads coped with the uncertainties in their life by developing a hyper-masculinity. A recent study by the Kirklees LEA (Noble 1999) in regard to male underachievement argues that this issue demands immediate attention.

They state that: 'to establish a generation of under-achieving, under-skilled and unemployed 16–24 males is a danger to society and its most vulnerable members who are often women' (Noble, 1999, p. 2).

We can see from the figures cited in the first section of this chapter that there are equal numbers of males and females at all attainment levels. Why then do some females underachieve? Perhaps some women define their career options in terms of having children.

Why do some beat the odds?

Some boys in the Mac an Ghaill (1994) study did not take on the role of the macho lads. These boys were described as developing a business-like masculinity. They took a realistic view of life and saw academic success as a way to get on and get out. Academic success would open up the possibilities of employment in newer jobs. In the previous section it was stated that certain ethnic minority groups were in fact over-represented in higher education. Mirza (1997) and Bryan *et al.* (1985) argue that discrimination in the workplace forces black students, both male and female, back to school and that the attainment of vocational qualifications is one way of fighting discrimination.

Why do some boys underachieve despite benefits from social class?

Aggleton (1987) studied a group of young people from the new middle class. Aggelton found that the young men studied had a definition of masculinity and achievement that differed from that of their parents. Here we again see a relationship between gender and academic achieve-ment. It would seem that students tend to define themselves first by their gender and that this gender identification will have an effect on how they define themselves as a learner (Noble 1999). The young men of the Aggleton study saw themselves as 'midway between the brutish manliness they associated with manual labour and the essential impotence they saw as characteristic of those whose involve-ment in mental labour was both committed and industrious' (Aggleton 1987, p. 73). 'In perceiving themselves as positioned between the macho lad and the sexless swot they aimed for effortless achievement' (Aggleton, 1987, p. 72). Of course to succeed without effort is a difficult task.

Strategies for improving educational performance

Strategies for raising boys' achievement

Noble (1999) reports on a programme started by Kirklees LEA in 1995, which aimed to raise boys' achievement. At that point there was a 12 per cent gap between boys' and girls' attainment levels at GCSE. Since the implementation of the programme the gap has reduced. The programme consists of a three-part plan:

1 *Raising awareness*
   - This involves talking not just with teachers, but with the wider school community to include parents and governors.
   - Boys need to be made aware of the issue of underachievement, but care needs to be taken in regard to how this is communicated. 'Telling boys that they are lazy, semi-literate and disruptive will only strengthen the anti-swot culture rather than challenge it . . . boys have to feel that it is not like them to under achieve and that it is actually errant male behaviour' (Noble 1999, p. 2).

2 *Whole school strategies*
   - Endeavouring to make Year 3 and Year 8 a particularly interesting and enriching experience.
   - Reviewing setting arrangements. 'Tight setting tends to depress academic achievements of boys and ethnic minority students' (Noble 1999, p. 2).
   - Emphasising literacy at all levels.
   - Working with parents. Asking some of the parents to work as potential role models for the school. 'Each department could prepare a leaflet describing how parents might use aspects of their environment and everyday life to give subjects relevance for their children' (Noble 1999, p. 3).
   - It is of utmost importance to portray the school as a learning environment. Teachers should take a lead role in this. 'How does the staff portray themselves as learners? Do the male teachers and support workers talk about what they have read recently and what they have learned? . . . Do teachers see themselves as learning about and from their students; or as sometimes getting it wrong and trying different approaches?' (Noble 1999, p. 3).

3 *Classroom strategies*
- Having a seating policy designed to maximise learning.
- Emphasis on learning styles. 'Engaging boys more by keeping teacher input as brief as possible, and cutting tasks down to small, bite sized chunks' (Noble 1999, p. 3).
- Adopting co-operative learning techniques such as 'shared writing'. 'Boys and girls like this. It gives them a sense of responsibility and the opportunity not merely of reflecting on their own work, but encouraging others also to reflect' (Noble 1999, p. 4).
- 'Teachers portraying themselves as learners, by asking the class at the end of the lesson when revisiting the learning objectives, how the lesson could have been improved' (Noble 1999, p. 4).

Raising Achievement Levels for Minority Ethnic Pupils (DfEE 2000b)

This document outlines four specific areas, which it feels as crucial to raising attainment.

1 *Raising expectations*
This involves the need for teachers, parents and students to believe in the students' potential and to value and celebrate their successes. High expectations regarding success are supported by:

- Programmes of mentoring and having pupils acting as role models.

> The mentoring programme in the school was extended specifically for Black male students in Years 9 and 10. The mentors were young men in their early twenties who had achieved, were from the local community and could relate to the students and speak to them about school.
>
> (DfEE 2000b, p. 10)

> One boy, S, was able to be popular, to work and still have credibility with the other students. We have lads like that who don't mind having their work pinned up or who don't mind being highlighted. One of S's friends came in and asked for extra work at KS3 because he wanted to do as well as S.
>
> (DfEE 2000b, p. 10)

- Structured learning and support programmes which include specific support for different areas of the curriculum, assessment and target setting, and a programme which respects the cultural background of all pupils.

> Students studied examples of Black writers writing in English.
>
> (DfEE 2000b, p. 14)

> One school explained that in teaching Macbeth they had made links with certain traditions in Islam.
>
> (DfEE 2000b, p. 14)

> African Studies was initially introduced in response to one group, the African Caribbean male students, whose behaviour was causing concern. Despite giving time to these extra initiatives, the school had progressively improved in terms of overall higher grades at GCSE.
>
> (DfEE 2000b, p. 14)

2 *Culture and ethos*
- Heads and governors to establish and effectively communicate values to which the whole school was committed.
- High standards of behaviour and a culture of mutual respect to be adopted by all.
- Systems of reprimand and reward that are recognised as fair to all to be implemented.
- Conscious attempts to be made to counter the effect of stereotyping and prejudice, and procedures implemented to deal with race relations.

3 *Parental involvement*
- Parental involvement to be encouraged by increased communication with staff, to include: designation of staff members whom they could telephone, home visits, open-door sessions and language assistance.

4 *Ethnic monitoring*
- The school needs a system to keep track and analyse what is happening for their ethnic minority pupils in regard to academic progress and behavioural issues.

Summary

Explaining gender and cultural diversity in educational achievement is not an easy task. Overall trends can be established. Girls have outperformed boys in attaining higher grades at GCSE. However overall trends can obscure differences in relation to subgroups and individuals within subgroups. As we have seen in this chapter, academic achievement depends on an interaction between a number of factors, including gender, social class, type of schooling, ethnic background, and how the individual sees educational achievement in relation to their gender identity and peer group. Strategies for raising academic standards were discussed in relation to boys and pupils from ethnic minorities. This is an area of ongoing concern and research.

1 Imagine that you have taken over an inner city comprehensive with 50 per cent of the students coming from ethnic minorities. Underachievement is an issue of concern for most students. GCSE results in the previous academic year were as follows:

Percentage of students achieving 5+ A*–C grades:

Boys 25%   Girls 33%

Review exercise

However, those who do well, do exceptionally well. On a breakdown of who does well it was revealed that ethnic background was not a factor.

Your school also has a history of having behavioural problems and an exclusion rate twice the LEA average.

Your task is:

(i) To come up with various explanations for underachievement and achievement.

(ii) To design a programme to raise standards. Good luck!!

2 Review the LEA league tables from your area. How do they compare with the statistics mentioned in this chapter?

Further reading

The following government publications are well worth a read.

Gillborn, D. and Gipps, C. (1996) *Recent Research on the Achievements of Ethnic Minority Pupils*, OFSTED Review of Research, London: HMSO.

Arnot, M., Gray, J., James, M. and Rudduck, J. (1998) *A Review of Recent Research on Gender and Educational Performance*, OFSTED Research Series, London: The Stationery Office. http://www.standards.dfee.gov.uk/genderandachievement

The Government Standards internet site is worth visiting for up-to-date information regarding academic results.

6

Learning and teaching styles

Introduction

When investigating issues regarding learning and teaching styles it is easy to become overwhelmed by the variety of terminology used and the quagmire of inventories and indexes available which claim to measure some aspect of your **learning style**. In regard to terminology, there are learning styles, cognitive styles, learning strategies, teaching styles and instructional strategies. It is hoped that by the end of this chapter the differences in terms of what these concepts mean will be apparent. This chapter will attempt to make sense of some theories of learning style, and address the limitations of measurement devices as well as exploring how learning and teaching styles can lead to an improvement in learning effectiveness.

Definitions

What is a learning style? Bennett (1990) stated that learning style is a

> consistent pattern of behaviour and performance by which an individual approaches educational experiences. It is the composite of characteristic cognitive, affective, and physiological behaviours that serve as relatively stable indicators of how a learner perceives, interacts with, and responds to the learning environment.
>
> (Bennett 1990, p. 140)

Dunn, Dunn and Price (1985) identified twenty-two elements relating to learning style. These elements are related to dimensions such as:

- *Environmental*: preferences regarding bright versus dim light; sound present or absent; cool versus warm temperature; and formal or informal classroom design.
- *Emotional*: individuals will differ on levels of persistence and motivation, and on issues such as degree of responsibility versus non-conformity.
- *Sociological*: preferences in relation to who to work with – that is, alone, in groups or in pairs.
- *Physical*: refers to perceptual strengths such as whether the individual is an auditory, visual or tactile learner. This measure would also include time-of-day preferences – that is, whether the individual prefers to learn in the morning or evening.
- *Psychological*: refers to such dimensions as whether the individual is impulsive or reflective (Griggs 1991).

Just to complicate issues, Riding and Cheema (1991) note the distinction between cognitive styles and learning styles, although they comment that many theorists will use these terms interchangeably. They would see cognitive style as underlying learning style and involving theoretical academic descriptions of processes involved, while learning style is more immediately apparent and of interest to trainers and educators.

Structure or process

Riding and Cheema (1991) further comment that learning style has been perceived in three ways:

1 *Structure* (content): learning style is seen to reflect a presumed stable structure which remains constant over time; therefore it is the task of an educator to determine what an individual's learning style is for that environment and to match or adapt the method of instruction to the learning style.
2 *Process*: learning style is seen as being in a state of continuous change, and therefore the focus should be on discovering how it changes and how an instructor can foster that change.
3 *Structure and process*: this view would see learning style as being relatively stable but at the same time being modified by events.

Curry's Onion Model

Curry's Onion Model of Learning Styles (Curry 1983) attempts to explain how learning style can be viewed as both a structure and a process, both relatively stable and at the same time open to modification. Curry's model argues that all learning-style measures may be placed into three groups or 'strata resembling layers of an onion':

1 *Outermost layer of the onion*: Curry refers to this as *instructional preference*, and of all measures of learning styles this is the most unstable. Learning environment and individual and teacher expectations can influence instructional preferences. An example of a learning-style measure at this level would be the 'Learning Preference Inventory' (Rezler and Rezmovic 1981).
2 *Middle layer of the onion*: Curry refers to this as the *informational processing style*. This learning style reflects the individual's intellectual approach to integrating or assimilating information. This type of learning style is more stable than instructional preferences but may still be influenced by learning strategies. An example of a learning-style measure at this level would be the 'Learning Style Inventory' (Kolb 1976).
3 *Innermost layer of the onion*: Curry refers to this as *cognitive personality style*, which is defined as the individual's approach to assimilating and adapting information. This dimension does not

99

interact with the environment, although this dimension fundamentally controls all learning behaviour. An example of a learning-style measure at this level would be the Myers-Briggs Type Indicator (Myers 1962).

Of interest in the above model is the implication that learning strategies can influence certain learning styles. A learning style is a fairly fixed and stable characteristic of an individual, whereas a learning strategy outlines a way to approach a situation, task or problem and may be learned and developed over time. Over the course of a lifetime an individual might learn many learning strategies, but their learning style will remain fairly constant (Riding and Cheema 1991).

Teaching style and instructional strategy

To add to this collection of definitions we also have the distinction between teaching style and instructional strategy. Bennett (1990) described a teacher's method or instructional strategy as their preference for lecture, small group work or oral reports, whereas 'teaching style refers to the teacher's pervasive personal behaviour and media used during interaction with learners. It is the teacher's characteristic approach whatever the method used' (Bennett 1990, p. 161). One example of a teaching style is a formal or an informal approach. A formal teaching style would focus on the subject to be taught and the responsibility of the teacher to impart this knowledge. An informal teaching style would emphasise the individual's specific learning needs and the teacher's responsibility to create the appropriate learning experiences.

Progress exercise 6.1

Match the following terms to the following definitions:

teaching style   learning styles   cognitive styles   learning strategy

1   Differences in perceptual strengths (visual or auditory learners) or differences in preferences regarding time to learn (morning vs. evening) are examples of _____.

2   _____ are academic descriptions of processes involved in learning which underlie learning styles.

3 A learning style is a fairly fixed and stable characteristic of an individual, whereas a way of remembering the following sequence ICIIBMCIAFBI by grouping the sequence into meaningful chunks such as ICI-IBM-CIA-FBI is an example of a _____, which can be learned.

4 _____ is described as a teacher's characteristic approach regardless of instructional strategy used.

(Answers can be found on p. 181)

Theories

There are many theories of or approaches to measuring learning styles. In this section we will concentrate on three theories.

Myers-Briggs Type Indicator (MBTI)

This theory would classify individuals' learning style according to four dimensions or scales. These scales were derived from Jung's theory of psychological types. The scales are shown in Table 6.1

Table 6.1 Myers-Briggs Type Indicator		
Extroverts Focus on outer world	vs.	*Introverts* Focus on inner world
Sensors Emphasis on facts and procedures	vs.	*Intuitors* Emphasis on meanings and possibilities
Thinkers Decisions are made on the basis of logic and rules	vs.	*Feelers* Decisions are made on the basis of personal considerations
Judgers Set and strictly follow agendas	vs.	*Perceivers* Can change with circumstances

According to this model, individual scores on these scales, in combination, form a total of sixteen different learning styles. For example, an individual could be an extrovert, sensor, thinker and judger (Felder 1996).

Kolb's Learning Style Inventory

Kolb (1976) saw the learning process as being separated into two distinct components: perception (how the information is taken in) and processing (how the information is internalised).

In terms of perception (how the information is taken in), an individual would either have a preference for:

Concrete experience: participating in specific situations. Relating to people with an emphasis on feeling.

or

Abstract conceptualisation: an emphasis on analysing, thinking and planning, rather than feeling.

In terms of processing (how the information is internalised), an individual would either have a preference for:

Active experimentation: preference for doing something with the information, emphasising risk taking and being involved in practical applications that influence people.

or

Reflective observation: preference for thinking about the information rather than doing, with an emphasis on understanding, searching for a meaning, and seeing the situation from different perspectives.

These two dimensions of perceiving and processing information result in four types of learners:

Type 1: (*concrete experience + reflective observation*)
Type 2: (*abstract conceptualisation + reflective observation*)
Type 3: (*abstract conceptualisation + active experimentation*)
Type 4: (*concrete experience + active experimentation*)

(Felder 1996, FEDA 1995)

The Honey and Mumford learning styles (1986)

Honey and Mumford adapted Kolb's theories and formulated a learning-style questionnaire. Honey and Mumford defined four learning styles:

Activist Functions in immediate present, prefers hands-on activities, loves challenges, gets bored with implementation, does not necessarily recognise problems.

Reflector Prefers to stand back and observe. Likes to think and analyse. Tends to be cautious.

Theorist Is rational, logical and analytic. Likes theories, models and order.

Pragmatist Likes new ideas. Excels at lateral thinking. Is keen to see if new ideas work in practice.

For each of the following students' comments, state what type of learning style you think the student has.

1 When I go into a lesson, I like to be involved. I like to jump right in and do something.

2 I like stimulating input! I love it when I hear a really interesting and thought-provoking lecture. I need time to digest and think about what I have heard. I don't like to be personally involved in the lesson and I don't like answering questions.

3 I like structure and order. When I go into a lesson I want to know what we are going to do, when we are going to do it and why we are going to do it.

4 I like activities in a lesson but there must be a reason for the activity, there must be a purpose to the activity.

(Answers on p. 181)

Progress exercise 6.2

Measurement of learning styles

Many indexes of learning styles are formulated on the basis of question-naires. Learning-style inventories are an example of a psychometric test and consequently will have certain advantages and limitations, as mentioned in Chapter 3.

Concerns regarding measurement of learning styles

- *Reliability*: there are issues regarding reliability or consistency in regard to scores on learning-style questionnaires. Test scores should not fluctuate with such factors as mood or time of day when the test was taken.
- *Validity*: the test should be valid, that is, it should measure what it sets out to measure, not other factors. Consideration needs to be given to question design. For example, if a questionnaire had asked for a response to the statement 'Do you like watching TV?', what would a response to that statement really tell us about an individual's learning style? Some questions on some learning-style question-naires will call for a *yes* or a *no* answer, but do *yes* or *no* answers really reflect how we feel regarding an issue?
- *Response bias*: do we answer the way we feel we should answer?
- *Are we aware of how we learn?* Are some individuals more aware of how they learn than others? Honey and Mumford (1992) felt that although individuals prefer different ways of learning most individuals were not aware of these preferences. Would degree of self-awareness affect the validity of a learning-style inventory?
- *Tendency to place individuals in discrete categories*: there is a danger of typecasting. Is it true that once an activist always an activist? Kolb (1984) states that the aim in identifying preferred learning styles should be to lead to greater choices, decisions and possibilities. Perhaps knowledge of personal learning styles (includ-ing strengths and limitations) and knowledge of other learning styles (including strengths and limitations) will encourage the individual to experiment with alternative learning styles.
- *How do the numerous indexes of learning styles relate to each other?* Learning-style inventories measure a range of variables. An individual could find out their learning styles in regard to room temperature, or time-of-learning preference, as well as to what degree they were an activist or a reflector. The question is: how does all this information fit together? Lewis (1976) states that many theorists seem 'determined to pursue their own pet distinctions in cheerful disregard of each other' (Lewis 1976, p. 304).

- *What is the relationship between learning styles and specific instructional styles?* Reiff (1992) states that although many learning styles have been identified, the usefulness of such information has yet to be established. Clear links between learning styles, specific educational environments and specific instructional approaches need to be set out.

Advantages of learning-style indexes

If learning styles can be ascertained, then instructional strategies can be geared to learning style, resulting in improvement in learning effectiveness. The next section in this chapter will look at studies that have tried to make links between learning styles, instructional strategies and improved performance.

Alternative methods of measuring learning style

As stated above, learning style is often measured by questionnaires, but are there other ways? If there is a match between learning styles and instructional strategies, then perhaps we only have to determine preferred instructional strategy to infer learning style. It would be possible to systematically present a number of instructional strategies to an individual and measure their performance on each, to determine what instructional strategy resulted in maximum performance.

The MADEUP learning-style inventory to differentiate between visual and auditory learners

(To each of the following, answer *yes* or *no*)

1 I always prefer reading rather than listening to the radio.

2 I would prefer that my teacher just talked rather than wrote information on the board.

3 When driving somewhere new do you make a tape-recording outlining step-by-step instructions of how to get there, and then listen to the tape when driving?

4 Reading makes my eyes sore.

Progress exercise 6.3

---

5   I like writing notes in class.

6   I find the notes on the OHP particularly helpful.

7   I prefer to tape-record what happens in class.

Scoring

If you answered yes to nos. 1, 5 and 6 you are a visual learner.

If you answered yes to nos. 2, 3, 4 and 7 you are an auditory learner.

Questions

1   How would you evaluate the MADEUP learning-style inventory?

2   Evaluate another learning-style inventory that you have used.

Individual differences in learning styles

In this section we will look at differential learning styles in relation to gender and ethnic minority groups. We will also look at possible individual differences in learning style in relation to autism. The studies mentioned are attempting to make links between learning style, instructional strategies and learning effectiveness. Of course, it is important to remember that although trends do emerge, they can and do obscure differences that exist within groups.

Gender

Boaler (1997) carried out a study which supported the view that boys and girls have preferences for different ways of 'knowing'. Boaler (1997) studied and tracked a group of Year 9 students in two different schools in regard to mathematical achievement for three years. The schools chosen were in similar areas and the students had similar scores on cognitive ability tests at the commencement of Year 9. The only difference between the two groups was the way in which maths was taught. In the first school, the approach was traditional, content-led and textbook-based. The second school had an approach that was open and project-based with an emphasis on process. After three years, differences in achievement were found between the two schools. Girls achieved less when taught with a traditional approach; this was most noticeable within the top sets. Interviews with students suggested a female preference for learning tasks that were open-ended, project-based, related to real situations and which gave time for thinking and discussion. Males, though preferring discussion, were more willing and better at adapting to traditional approaches which required memorising abstract facts and rules. Arnot *et al.* (1998) on evaluating this study note that generalisations based on such a small study would be dangerous; however the hypothesis of gender differences in learning styles deserves further testing.

Autism

Edelson (2000) writes regarding the learning styles of students with autism, specifically their preference for visual (learning through see-ing), auditory (learning through hearing) or kinaesthetic (learning by touching) modes. Edelson and colleagues believe that many autistic individuals rely on only one style of learning; therefore a careful assessment of preferred learning styles could lead to more appropriate teaching interventions. Edelson states that one common problem cited by teachers involves difficulties with autistic students running around the classroom in disregard of teacher instruction. Edelson comments that perhaps such a student is not an auditory learner and teacher instruction should be based on another modality or learning style. Perhaps a kinaesthetic approach (placing a hand on the child's shoulders and guiding the child to his chair) or a visual approach (showing the child a picture of a chair and gesturing to him to sit on it) would be more effective. If in doubt regarding preferred learning style then it is advisable to teach concepts using all modalities.

Ethnic minority groups

Griggs and Dunn (1996) write on the learning styles of various ethnic minorities, with specific reference to Hispanic American students. Learning style was looked at from five dimensions and the following differences were noted:

1 *Environmental learning style*. It was noted that Mexican-American elementary and middle school pupils preferred a cool temperature and a formal classroom design.

2 *Emotional learning style*. This learning style referred to respon-sibility, structure, persistence and motivation. It would seem that Mexican-Americans require a higher degree of structure than other groups.

3 *Sociological learning style*. More Caucasian students preferred working alone than either Mexican-American children or African-American children, with African-American children expressing the greatest preference for group work (Dunn and Dunn 1992, Sims 1988).

4 *Physiological learning style*. Puerto-Rican college students exhibited a strong preference for learning in the late morning onwards. Sims (1988) found that Caucasian students preferred eating and drinking while studying significantly more than Mexican-Americans. Caucasians and African-Americans were significantly more auditory and visual in their learning style than Mexican-Americans. Latinos were rated as kinaesthetic learners (Yong and Ewing 1992, Dunn, Griggs and Price 1993).

Griggs and Dunn (1996) state that it is important to be aware of the limitations of such research and to appreciate that individual learning style will be affected by many variables, ethnic background being just one. Learning style will also be influenced by socio-economic status, region, religion, family structure, etc. However, noting the limitations of such research, Hispanic students on the whole prefer a cool environ-ment, peer-orientated learning, and kinaesthetic instructional resources, and have energy peaks in the late morning and afternoon.

Improving learning effectiveness and study skills

There are various strategies that claim to raise achievement. These strategies themselves could be categorised as follows:

- Strategies that attempt to match learning styles with instructional approaches.
- Teaching of specific study skills such as time management and note-taking skills, and steps involved in researching and improving reading techniques.

- Meta-cognitive approaches: teaching learners how to learn. This would include thinking skills programmes such as Feuerstein's Instrumental Enrichment and Process Based Instruction.

From learning styles to instructional approaches

Given that we have identified an individual's learning style, what should happen next? If a teacher realises that they are not teaching to the individual's preferred learning style, should they change or adapt the material? What if the demands of the curriculum necessitate whole group teaching? What if each student in the class has a different learning style? One way of getting around this issue would be to use various instructional strategies which aim to teach to some of the students' preferred learning styles at least some of the time. This approach would also work if you didn't know what the students' learning styles were. Taking a different viewpoint, Felder (1996) argues that if a teacher teaches exclusively to the student's preferred learning style then the student 'may not develop the mental dexterity they need to reach their potential for achievement in school and professions, where they will need to be flexible in their approach to learning' (Felder 1996, p. 18).

4-MAT system

McCarthy (1990) took Kolb's learning-style descriptions and modified them to create the '4-MAT system', which is used in designing and developing classroom lesson plans for students ranging from 5 to 17. From Kolb's model, McCarthy outlined four types of learners and eight aspects of lesson design (as outlined in Table 6.2).

McCarthy argues that each learning style has its own strengths and weaknesses and that this method of lesson presentation allows each student to experience their preferred way of learning as well as working through other ways of learning. This method of lesson planning would give all students valuable experience in all learning styles. But what does this system look like in practice? At this point it is helpful to look at a specific example.

Table 6.2 4-MAT system

Kolb's model	McCarthy's type of learner	Aspect of lesson plan
Concrete experience	*Innovative/imaginative* The student perceives information by feeling and sensing. These individuals need to reflect on their experiences.	*Motivation* This aspect of the lesson is geared to those students who need to be actively involved. These students need to know why the information is relevant and how it is related to their existing experiences. The motivation aspect of the lesson would be divided into: • Create the experience. • Reflect on the experience.
Reflective observation	*Analytic* The individual student processes information by watching and thinking and then proceeds to develop theories.	*Concept development* This aspect of the lesson is geared to those students who like to have information presented to them in the form of what the experts say, or what the text states. The concept development part of the lesson would be divided into: • Integrate reflections into concepts. • Present and develop theories and concepts.

Abstract conceptualisation	*Common sense* The individual first formulates and develops theories, then needs to know whether they work in practice.	*Practice* This aspect of the lesson allows the students to understand the information presented in the previous stage through practical exercises and activities. This aspect of the lesson is divided into: • Practise and reinforce new information. • Personalise the experience.
Active experimentation	*Dynamic* The individual student learns by feeling and sensing and then by experimenting with ways in which they can use this information.	*Application* This aspect of the lesson would have students exploring ways in which information learned can be applied to new situations. This aspect of the lesson is divided into: • Develop a plan for applying new concepts. • Do it and share it with others.

Example of the 4-MAT approach to lesson planning

Aim of the lesson: to teach learning styles to a class of learning support assistants.

Motivation

1 *Create the experience*

Students are asked to design what they consider to be the perfect lesson plan for the topic 'The truth behind UFOs'.

2 *Reflect on the experience*

Students are asked to get into groups and to compare their ideas on what they consider to be the perfect lesson plan.

Concept development

3 *Integrate reflection into concepts*

A general discussion is held to compare and contrast lesson plans. The theme that would be developed, through discussion, would make connections between differences in ideal lesson plans and individual preferred learning styles.

4 *Present and develop theories and concepts*

A handout of learning styles includes Kolb's, Honey and Mumford's and McCarthy's theories. The handout is discussed.

Practice

5 *Practise and reinforce new information*

The students are required to complete Honey and Mumford's learning-style inventory.

6 *Personalise the experience*

The students are requested to get into groups and discuss what they have found out in regard to their unique learning style.

Application

7 *Develop a plan for applying new concepts*

Students are told to get into small groups and in their groups to develop a lesson plan for the topic 'The truth behind UFOs', using the 4-MAT system.

8 *Do it and share it with others*

A member of each group presents their lesson plan to the class. The class discusses issues such as whether it will work and whether it will work with all students.

Bowers (1987) investigated the effect of a 4-MAT system on fifty-four gifted Year 6 students. The students were randomly assigned to either a 4-MAT group or a Restricted-Textbook group. Both groups were taught a unit on Newton's First Law of Motion. A test was given at the end of the unit. Significant differences were found on overall scores and critical thinking scores in favour of the 4-MAT system.

Sangster and Shulman (1988) studied a pilot programme involving the implementation and evaluation of the 4-MAT curriculum in secondary schools. Thirty-one teachers and 572 students were involved. Questionnaires and interviews revealed that both students and teachers perceived the system favourably.

Study skills

There has been a wealth of information regarding how to study more effectively. These include tips for organising your time, improving your reading technique, how to take notes in class, how to write essays and how to revise for exams. In terms of time management, Johnson, Springer and Sternglanz (1982) recommend the following:

- Set aside times and places for work.
- Set priorities and follow them.
- Break larger tasks into smaller ones.
- Do not overwhelm yourself with tasks; be reasonable in regard to how many tasks you can do in a day.
- Work on one thing at a time.
- Check your progress often.

Robinson (1970) developed the SQ3R method of effective reading.

1 *Survey*: before you start to read a chapter, try to get an overview of what information the chapter is presenting. Read chapter outlines. Look at the various headings.
2 *Question*: for every heading presented in the chapter, convert it into a question. Asking questions will help you to become more involved in your reading.
3 *Read*: read one specific section at a time. Read the section with the aim of answering the question you have just formulated.

4 *Recite*: recite the answer to the question out loud (if possible) and in your own words. You might want to make notes at this point. Keep repeating steps 2–4 until you have finished reading the chapter.

5 *Review*: when you have finished the chapter, go back over key points and questions.

Evaluation of study skills programmes

Leland-Jones (1997) investigated the use of a study skills programme in raising academic achievement in Year 6 students. A unit of study skills emphasising the use of resource material, interpreting data and creating chapter outlines was incorporated into individual chapters on a social studies course. The programme resulted in increased knowledge of study skills and higher achievement scores.

Brown and Forristall (1983) investigated the use of a 'Computer-Assisted Study Skills Improvement Program'. The computer program provided interactive instruction on topics such as time management, improving memory, taking lecture notes and reading textbooks. Students completing the program showed significant improvement in study skill and academic abilities.

One scheme that aims to encourage study skills is called 'Playing for Success'. This scheme targets underachieving young people in Key Stages 2 and 3 within inner city areas, and establishes the study support centres in English Premiership and First Division football clubs. Using the environment of football, the centres focus on skills in literacy and numeracy. The centres also provide opportunities for pupils to develop ICT and study skills and to complete their homework. Evaluation indicates that as many girls as boys participate and that both boys and girls benefit equally in terms of attitudes and improved reading and maths abilities (Sharp *et al.* 1999).

Meta-cognitive approaches

Meta-cognition involves our personal awareness of factors that influence our own thinking, learning and problem-solving abilities. It is argued that the more we know about the process of learning, the more we can incorporate this knowledge into our own learning, thus becoming more independent and efficient. This view stresses the role of the learner as being actively involved in the learning process. There are a number approaches in this area such as Feuerstein's Instrumental Enrichment and Process Based Instruction.

Feuerstein's Instrumental Enrichment

Key to this programme are the concepts of 'structured cognitive modifiability' and 'mediated learning experiences'. This programme places an emphasis on both the emotional and cognitive factors underlying learning. A central role within the programme is that of the teacher who places themselves between the child and the environment in order to control and interpret incoming stimuli in order to promote a greater understanding of the environment. This process is described as mediated learning experiences, with the teacher as the mediator (Feuerstein *et al.* 1980). Successful mediation requires the teacher to ensure that students:

- Understand what they are supposed to do.
- Understand why they are doing the task.
- Appreciate that the task has value or applications beyond the here and now of the classroom.
- Develop an appreciation of what they can realistically do, an awareness of when they need help and the skills necessary to ask for help.
- Through the above goals, are encouraged in skills of self-reflection and awareness of inner thoughts and feelings.

It is through these mediated learning experiences that underlying cognitive structures are modified or changed.

Process Based Instruction

This programme (Ashman and Conway 1993) aims to teach students how to learn and solve problems through the development of meta-cognitive strategies. The programme focuses on four components, which aim to promote skills such as self-questioning, decision making and evaluation (see Table 6.3).

Doran and Cameron (1995) state that these skills should be taught, commencing in reception classrooms.

Table 6.3 Four components of Process Based Instruction

Component	Skills taught
Cueing	Where to start and how to start.
Acting	The sequences of actions needed.
Monitoring	How to review whether the plan is working as expected.
Verifying	How to determine whether the task has been completed correctly or whether to go back and try again.

Progress exercise 6.4

A Year 7 student has been given an assignment of writing two pages on a famous scientist. Using the Process Based Instruction approach, what advice would you give a student who just doesn't know what to do regarding this assignment?

Summary

In this chapter we have looked at various definitions including: learning styles, cognitive styles, learning strategies, teaching styles and instructional strategies. We have looked at three theories regarding learning styles: Kolb's, Honey and Mumford's and the MBTI. As learning styles are often measured by an individual completing a questionnaire, various points of concern were raised. Some research concerned with revealing differential learning styles in relation to gender and ethnic minority groups was discussed. What has emerged from this short introduction to the field of teaching and learning styles is not only the potential benefits of matching learning styles to instructional strategies, but also the real need for further research in this area.

1   What does the research say in regard to improving learning effectiveness?

2   There are an incredible number of learning-style inventories or indexes available. Your task is to find and complete as many as possible. The internet is a good place to search. After completing as many inventories as possible, what have you found out about yourself?

Further reading

Further Education Development Agency (1995) *Learning Styles*. This short booklet looks at Honey and Mumford's model of learning styles in considerable depth. The advantage of this booklet is that it has a copy of the learning-style questionnaire, adapted for 16–19-year-olds, in the appendix.

The National Foundation for Educational Research (Nfer) is a valuable source for information regarding current projects. The Nfer has a very useful internet site with many publications available. This is one of my favourite sites: http://www.nfer.ac.uk/

An interesting site for those interested in more information regarding study skills is: http://www.utexas.edu/student/lsc/ststr.html

Motivation

Introduction

Motivation is a word that is often used in a number of contexts. We see newspaper advertisements seeking enthusiastic, self-motivated individuals. When we say that a top athlete was really up for the game, we are in a sense saying that he was highly motivated. When we tell our friends that we just couldn't face the thought of doing our assignment or getting down to revising for that exam, we are describing our lack of motivation. But what is motivation? What can we do to improve our motivation? This chapter will attempt to answer these questions.

Definitions

Simply put, motivation deals with the whys of behaviour. Theories of motivation are often based on the assumption that there are no random acts of behaviour, but that everything we do, we do for a reason. Freud would further stipulate that although there are always reasons (motives) for behaviour we might not consciously be aware of why we do what we do.

Cohen (1990) defined motivation as that something that drives people to do what they do. Brehm and Self (1989) felt that it was too simple to say that someone is either motivated or not motivated. They believed that it was more helpful to think of motivation in terms of the extent to which we are motivated, or how much effort we are willing to put into an activity. The extent to which we are motivated depends on our internal needs, potential outcomes and our personal estimation regarding how likely it is that our behaviour will lead to desired outcomes.

Like many concepts in psychology, defining motivation proves complex. In addition to these definitions regarding motivation there are certain questions we need to ask:

- Are there different forms or types of motivation?
- What role do others have in developing our motivation?

Certainly the role of others in developing motivation is central to teaching and education. Taylor and Thornton (1995, p. 16) state that: 'No one is responsible for the motivation of another person.' Professionals such as teachers cannot control the motivation of their students but can only act in ways most likely to influence motivation, for the good or otherwise. So whatever motivation is, it is not something that we can give, but only influence.

Types

When theorists talk about different types of motivation, they are making connections between observed behaviour and presumed reasons, or motives, which underlie that behaviour. There are many different types of motivation.

- *Physiological/psychological*: on a very basic level we could talk about physical or physiological needs. Physiological needs would include food, water, rest and sex. Psychological needs, on the other hand, would relate to mental and social activities. For every designated need there is a presumed motivation to meet that need.

- *Competence*: White (1959) observed how developing children actively explored their environment. White felt that this innate exploratory behaviour was a result of an individual's need to exert an influence on their environment. This need corresponded to what White (1959) termed effectance motivation, competence motivation or mastery motivation.
- *Achievement/competition*: our society is competitive; we compete against each other for grades, jobs, partners, etc. McClelland *et al.* (1953) talked of the need for achievement, or an achievement motivation. Harter (1981) stated that motivation to achieve could result from either a need for competency or mastery (intrinsic orientation), or a desire to earn external rewards such as good grades, prizes and praise (extrinsic orientation).
- *Affiliation*: another important psychological motivation is the desire to form attachments or the need to affiliate or interact with other individuals (Sigelman and Shaffer 1991).

As with many motivations, individuals will differ on the extent to which they possess a certain need or motivation. Therefore some individuals can be said to have a high achievement motivation and to be driven to succeed, to outperform others and to take on increasingly demanding challenges. Others who might have less of a need to achieve might be content just to get by.

Of course if different behaviours are determined by varying levels of motivations or needs, do these needs or motivations ever conflict? Would the need to affiliate conflict with the need to achieve?

From a teacher's viewpoint, can one type of motivation be better than another?

Theories

Drive theories

Some of the earliest research into motivation centred on biological needs such as hunger and thirst. These theories saw motivation in terms of need states and drive activities. The organism would first recognise that there was a deficiency, or a need; this would trigger a drive activity or a tendency to behave in such a manner as to reach the goal stimulus, which in turn would reduce the need (Hull 1943). This theory would make sense when talking about physiological needs such as why we eat, but would it make sense when applied to psychological needs such as the need for affiliation or achievement? LeFrancois (1997) notes that, whereas physiological needs can be satisfied, psychological needs are never completely satisfied.

The role of arousal: the Yerkes-Dodson Law

Without a doubt there is a physiological component to motivation. Arousal can be defined as changes in heart rate, brain activity and respiration. The psychological component of arousal would be reflected in the degree of focused attention. The assumption is that arousal can be roughly equated with motivation, usually with more arousal resulting in greater levels of motivation, but not always (Brehm and Self 1989). There is also an assumed belief that greater levels of arousal lead to greater levels of motivation, which in turn lead to greater levels of achievement. The **Yerkes-Dodson Law** states that there is a relationship between level of arousal, complexity of task and effectiveness of performance (see Figure 7.1).

A certain level of arousal is necessary for effective performance; however, too little or too much arousal can lead to ineffective performance. The level of arousal necessary for effective performance will vary with task complexity.

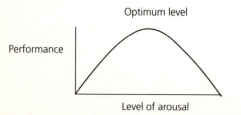

Figure 7.1 **The Yerkes-Dodson Law**

Analyse the following responses according to the Yerkes-Dodson Law.

Martin phoned in for 'Who Wants to be a Millionaire'. Martin can't believe it. He is now actually on the show. He is playing for £32,000. He has used up all his lifelines. If he gets the question right he leaves the show with £32,000; if he is wrong, he leaves the show with £1,000. Should he play or take the cheque? Is he confident? Is he sure?

The question is: who was the first Prime Minister of Canada?

(a) Black Adder   (b) John A. MacDonald

(c) Pierre Trudeau   (c) John McKenzie King

• What factors will affect Martin's performance?

(Hint: consider his level of arousal and task complexity.)

Humanistic theories

Although we share basic needs, such as the need for food and water, with non-human animals, our needs are more complex. Once our basic needs are met, we are driven by progressively higher levels of motivation. Theorists such as Maslow saw the reasons behind behaviour as stemming from intrinsic motives of becoming self-aware and realising one's potential. Maslow (1954) formulated a hierarchy of human needs (see Table 7.1).

Maslow's theory was hierarchical in the sense that more basic needs needed to be met before time and space were given over to achieving other higher needs. But is this always true? Slater (1996) talks of Maslow's model with reference to the treatment of schizophrenics. It has been assumed that 'love and intimacy must be preceded by adequate shelter and a stable mind relatively free from interpersonal or intrapsychic threats', but in her work with schizophrenics Slater claims to have witnessed glimmers of intimacy (Slater 1996, p. 10). This would seem to suggest that perhaps needs do not have to be met in such a linear fashion.

Other humanistic psychologists have defined other needs. Rogers (1961) talks of the need for self-regard. Harré (1979) talks of the need for social respect.

Table 7.1 Maslow's hierarchy of needs
7 *Self-actualisation* (need to realise one's potential)
6 *Aesthetic needs* (beauty, order, art)
5 *Cognitive needs* (curiosity, exploration, understanding, knowledge)
4 *Esteem needs* (respect, achievement, self-esteem)
3 *Belongingness* (receiving and giving love and affection)
2 *Safety needs* (security, protection, shelter)
1 *Physiological needs* (food, water, activity, rest, sex)

Cognitive theories and self-efficacy

Cognitive theories in regard to motivation would emphasise the thinking processes involved. **Self-efficacy** is a concept coined by Bandura (1986) which describes that part of the self that specifically relates to our estimation in regard to our personal effectiveness. It has been found that students with high estimates of personal effectiveness in regard to education, or a high level of academic efficacy, display greater persistence, effort, motivation and intrinsic interest in their education (Zimmerman, Bandura and Martinez-Pons 1992). From the point of view of a teacher, the next question is how do you instil a high level of self-efficacy in your students? In an attempt to answer this question we need to look at the various components of self-efficacy. Self-efficacy can be broken down into two aspects:

- Actual competencies or skills required for successful performance.
- Our estimation of our personal expertise in these competencies.

A person's perception of actual skills needed and their expertise in regard to these skills is very subjective. Bandura (1986), in acknowledging the subjective nature of these evaluations, outlined four factors that influence our evaluations:

- *Enactive*: these factors result from one's own actions. This is not as straightforward as it might appear, as success or failure is subject to personal interpretation or attribution. For example, a success might be put down to luck, while failure might be attributed to an incompetent teacher.
- *Vicarious*: these influences involve the individual looking around at how others have done and making comparisons. The most important comparisons a student makes are with their peers.
- *Persuasory*: for individuals who feel they are not competent at certain skills, statements of belief and encouragement from important others, such as parents and teachers, can be internalised within the individual and, it is hoped, serve as encouragement.
- *Emotive*: this involves the emotional intensity or arousal that we bring to a task. A certain amount of arousal will lead to increased attention but extreme levels of arousal, such as intense fear, can result in an individual being incapable of attempting the task.

The concept of self-efficacy is crucial as it determines what an individual chooses to do and the amount of effort that they expend in the task, or their motivation to engage in the task. The higher the level of self-efficacy, the greater the individual's persistence in the face of difficulty. From a teacher's perspective, the issue is, to what extent can you influence these personal evaluations?

Behaviourist theories

Cox (1991) writes on the motivation used by the coach who wishes to get the best out of their athletes. However, his views can equally be applied to the teaching profession. Cox (1991) sees motivation as a drive which can be influenced and purposefully changed by well-thought-out environmental manipulations, and in that sense his views are in line with behaviourist thinking (see Chapter 2). Cox (1991) talks of primary and secondary motivation and positive and negative motivation. Primary motivation is derived from the activity itself. In a classroom, examples of primary motivation might be the motivation derived from attending a lesson, writing an essay or doing coursework. Secondary motivation is any form of influence, except those associated directly with engaging in the activity itself. Examples of secondary motivation could be praise from parents, teachers and peers, certificates given and prizes awarded. Cox (1991) further states that the complexity of motivation stems from the fact that both primary and secondary sources of motivation can be perceived as either positive or negative. In terms of primary motivation the feedback for the student is the self-assessed value of the activity, or the self-assessed interpretation of their performance of that activity derived from a reflection on internal thoughts or emotions. Secondary motivation can be seen as positive or negative in terms of the feedback from secondary sources. At this stage it would help to have some specific examples. Let us imagine a student endeavouring to write a 2,000-word essay. Table 7.2 outlines how Cox's types of motivation can be applied to an essay writing task.

Table 7.2 Cox's types of motivation

Primary positive motivation This would see a student working on an essay, the ideas flowing from the student's mind on to the written page. The student would be saying: 'This is a hard topic, but I am enjoying writing this and the essay is really coming together.'	*Primary negative motivation* This would see the student getting bogged down writing the essay, crumpling up many sheets of paper and thinking: 'I just can't do this. I am hopeless! I don't know why I even bothered to do this course!'
Secondary positive motivation This would see the student receiving the essay back with the following comments: 'Well done! A well-organised essay with considered arguments for both sides of the essay – 20/25.'	*Secondary negative motivation* This would see the student receiving the essay back with the following comments: 'A very disappointing essay! You missed the point altogether. You must try harder – 8/25.'

Cox (1991) asserts that there is a complex ongoing relationship between motivation and feedback. As Cox states:

> We are motivated to do things and having done them receive feedback from a number of sources which we interpret positively or negatively. This interpretation affects our motivation to do them again immediately or in the future.
>
> (Cox 1991, p. 16)

Attribution theory

Weiner (1974, 1986) proposed an **attribution theory** which examined how an individual interpreted success or failure. The explanations we give ourselves for our successes or failures will determine our expectations of experiencing future successes or failures and consequently our motivation to engage in tasks where success or failure is a possible outcome.

Weiner's thinking built on earlier work by Rotter (1966). Rotter developed the concept of locus of control. **Locus of control** refers to the individual's beliefs regarding the relationship between their behaviour and subsequent rewards or punishments. An individual with an internal locus of control would see the consequences of their behaviour (rewards or punishments) as resulting from their own efforts. They would assume personal responsibility for what happened to them. In contrast, an individual with an external locus of control would see the consequences of their behaviour as a result of chance, fate, luck or as the result of the actions of others. These individuals would not see the consequences of their behaviour, regardless of whether they were good or bad, as a result of their own abilities or efforts. Locus of control should be seen as a continuum, with most individuals displaying beliefs somewhere between these two extremes (Corsini and Auerbach 1996).

Back to attribution theory. Weiner (1986) proposes that causal attribution, how an individual interprets success or failure, is made along two dimensions:

- internal vs. external causes
- stable vs. unstable causes

Table 7.3 demonstrates this classification system with an example of how a student might interpret receiving a good mark.

Table 7.3 Locus of causality

Example: Joe has received 98% for his maths test

	Internal cause	External cause
Stable cause	Ability (I have a flair for maths)	Task difficulty (The test was easy for me, though the others said it was incredibly difficult.)
Unstable Cause	Effort (I enjoy spending hours revising for maths tests!)	Luck (I don't need luck!)

Source: Adapted from Sigelman and Shaffer 1991, p. 381.

Progress exercise 7.2

How would an individual who has failed miserably explain his failure according to Weiner's attribution theory? (To help you with your answer fill in the following grid.)

	Internal cause	External cause
Stable Cause	Ability	Task difficulty
Unstable cause	Effort	Luck

Research has shown that high achievers attribute successes to internal and stable causes (high ability). Further, high achievers attribute failures to external and stable causes (test was not fair) or internal and unstable causes (I didn't really try, but next time I will do better)

(Dweck and Leggett 1988). High achievers who have the above attributional style are termed 'mastery orientated' in that their attributional style leads them to persist in the face of failure (Dweck and Leggett 1988). Individuals who tend to be low achievers often attribute their successes to internal unstable causes such as effort (I passed because I studied hard), or external causes such as 'the test was easy' or 'I was just lucky'. The key point is that these individuals do not make the connection between personal ability and success, even when they do succeed. However, when they fail they do make the connection between personal ability and consequences, and label themselves as thick and useless. As these individuals have low expectations regarding future successes, they have lower levels of motivation and tend to give up. Dweck (1978) has described this attributional style as a form of **learned helplessness**.

Learned helplessness

This term is derived from studies conducted by Seligman and Maier (1967) who exposed dogs to unavoidable electric shocks for a prolonged period of time. What Seligman and Maier discovered was that even when the conditions changed and the dogs could escape the electric shock they did not do so. It was speculated that the dogs had learned that whatever they did had no consequences for their environment; therefore they did nothing. This was referred to as learned helplessness. Seligman (1975) went on to make links between learned helplessness and the apathy experienced in depression. Individuals who are depressed believe that whatever they do doesn't matter.

How does learned helplessness relate to the concept of motivation? One could argue that if you truly believed that nothing you did mattered, then your motivation to try would be extremely low or non-existent (Hayes 1994). Learned helplessness could also influence your self-esteem. Renshaw (1990) in fact defined chronic low self-esteem as 'learned helplessness'. Given that an individual is experiencing learned helplessness, what can be done?

If learned helplessness is due to a faulty attributional style, as Dweck (1978) claimed, then perhaps attributional training will help. If learned helplessness is due to the belief that one has no control over one's environment, then perhaps encouraging greater participation, including making choices and decisions and setting personal targets, will help.

If learned helplessness is due to chronic low self-esteem, then measures to boost self-esteem might help. Of course all efforts to reduce learned helplessness will serve to increase motivation.

Improving motivation and reducing learned helplessness

Behaviourist interventions

Cox (1991) advocates behavioural techniques, such as shaping, choosing appropriate practices and activities that allow complete beginners to be successful. Here we see the relationship between outcomes and the future likelihood of engaging in the behaviour that led to such outcomes. This approach would encourage not only individuals who already have the ability but also those who have the potential. Cox focuses on the importance of verbal feedback which would form secondary motivation. Cox suggests:

1 Avoid value statements such as: 'That's great!' Such statements do not tell the student specifically what was great. When giving value statements make sure the students understand the reasons for it. Praise needs to be genuine and perceived as genuine.
2 Phrase corrective feedback in a positive framework. For instance, say 'try and do this', rather than 'don't do that'.
3 Impart criticism privately and avoid the embarrassment for the student of being put down in front of his peer group.
4 Give feedback as soon as possible.

Cox's guidelines for enhancing motivation rely heavily on basic behaviour modification techniques as put forward by Skinner. However, in Cox's guidelines we can detect the influence of other theoretical views in his approach. A person-centred approach is reflected in the need for empathy in order to recognise the effects of positive and negative motivation. The need for empathy implies that there should be opportunities set aside for teachers and students to communicate. The emphasis on the students' thinking processes highlights the cognitive approach to motivation. Perhaps, to improve motivation, a combination of techniques needs to be used.

Attributional training

Dweck (1975) conducted an attribution retraining treatment with children who she described as having become helpless in the face of repeated failures in maths. One group of 'helpless' children received training sessions, which always resulted in success. However, another group of 'helpless' children received training sessions, in which most sessions resulted in successes but some sessions were deliberately pre-arranged to end in failure. After these failing experiences the instructors told the children that they had not worked fast enough or tried hard enough. These two groups of children were then compared. Dweck was interested in the children's attitudes to failure. Interestingly the children who had experienced failure now attributed subsequent failure to internal unstable causes (that is, lack of effort), and consequently performed much better on maths problems. In contrast, the children who had never experienced failure continued to attribute subsequent failure to internal and stable causes (low ability), and remained firm in the belief that they couldn't do maths. This seems to be a key argument *against* **errorless learning**, in that students need to develop positive ways of dealing with failure in order to sustain high levels of motivation.

Involvement in target setting

One way of combating learned helplessness and increasing motivation would be to increase a student's involvement in the learning task. This can be achieved by encouraging student involvement in setting goals or targets.

Cox (1991) elaborates on the importance of negotiating goals and having several goals, and on the need for the goals to be within the individual's control. It is important to let individuals set their own goals. If the teacher sets them, then the students could see themselves as performing for others and this could lead to fear of failure, specifically the fear of falling short of others' expectations.

Rose *et al.* (1999) report on a study that aimed to encourage pupils with severe learning disabilities to become involved in setting personal goals and targets. Observations revealed 'considerable discrepancies in the pupil understanding of the process, and their ability to play a full part as target planners' (Rose *et al.* 1999, p. 208). This in turn led to a reflection on what component skills make up the ability of target setting. Individuals with learning disabilities have historically had less control over their lives and have been at greater risk of developing depression and learned helplessness than the normal population. As such, skills in making choices and decision making are vital for this group.

Specific programmes

Bleach and Smith (1998) report on a research project which explored factors influencing motivation and achievement in regard to boys' performance in English. As we have stated (see Chapter 5), boys' underachievement in English is an area of concern. Various ways forward were suggested. The use of preferred instructional style – including role-play, practical investigations and the use of information technology – was seen to increase motivation. Praise was recommended to raise future expectations of success and self-esteem. It was found that being keen in regard to studying English at school did not enhance boys' credibility with their peers. Here we see a conflict between the motivation for affiliation and the motivation for achievement. The authors state: 'a cool approach to the subject of boys' achievement is essential. As they grow older many prefer to play down the effort they make and cultivate an image of reluctant involvement, while still doing well' (Bleach and Smith 1998, p. 4).

Certainly there is sometimes a conflict between motives. Coleman (1961) asked high school students how they would like to be remembered. The results were as follows:

- 31 per cent of boys and 28 per cent of girls wanted to be remembered for their academic achievement.
- 45 per cent of boys wanted to be known for their athletic prowess and 24 per cent wanted to be popular.
- 37 per cent of girls wanted to be remembered for being leaders of extracurricular activities and 35 per cent wanted to be popular.

Coleman (1961) states that, since peer acceptance is highly valued, it is not surprising that students place more emphasis on social rather than academic goals. This study is certainly dated, but it demonstrates that the conflict between peer acceptance and academic achievement is a long-standing one. However, it could be argued that academic qualifications are more important in the twenty-first century than they were in the 1960s. If this is true how does a teacher motivate students to achieve? How do teachers take a 'cool approach' to subject delivery and achievement?

Summary

The concept of motivation attempts to explain why we engage in certain behaviours. Psychologists have developed many theories to explain motivation. Drive theories state that the organism experiences some sort of deficiency or need which triggers behaviour to rectify this need. Behaviourist theories see motivation as being shaped by environmental factors and influences. Humanistic theories focus on higher-level intrinsic motives reflecting a desire to self-actualise. On the other hand, cognitive theories focus on the thought processes involved. Related to motivation is attribution theory. Attribution theory deals with how we interpret success or failure. Our interpretation of past events will influence our motivation to engage in similar events in the future. Learned helplessness can be seen as a state where motivation to engage in adaptive behaviour is extremely low or non-existent.

To motivate students, or to have well-motivated students, is a concern to teachers. However, it would seem that motivation is something we cannot give to another but only influence. The question then becomes: how do we influence an individual so that an improvement in motivation results? To this end, methods such as attribution training, behaviouristic interventions and promoting greater participation were discussed.

Review exercise

An English department in a local secondary school is concerned about boys' underachievement. The department head wishes to devise a programme to increase motivation. What would you suggest?

(Hint: it might be helpful to consider attribution training, self-efficacy, and behaviourist interventions.)

Further reading

LeFrancois, G.R. (1997) *Psychology for Teaching*, Belmont, Calif.: Wadsworth. This book has a very interesting and informative chapter on motivation.

Hayes, N. (1994) *Foundations of Psychology*, London: Routledge. The chapter on motivation within this book is well worth the read.

8

Disruptive behaviour in school

Introduction
Definitions and types
Effects
Diagnosis
Explanations/causes/interventions
Summary

Introduction

The newspapers are full of headlines about students who are out of control and creating havoc in schools across the country. The person on the street might refer to such students as disruptive, unruly, rude juvenile delinquents lacking respect for authority. Those of us who are older will remember a time when there were severe consequences for acting out at school and that often the consequences took the form of physical punishment such as the strap, the cane, a ruler across the knuckles or a flying chalk brush. Society has moved on and the days of corporal punishment are long gone; however, disruptive behaviour within the classroom is still an issue. Teachers, psychologists and other professionals now refer to such disruptive behaviour as 'challenging behaviour' or **emotional behavioural difficulties**. The many views in regard to definitions, types, causes and suitable interventions for such behaviour are the focus of this chapter.

Definitions and types

As stated above, disruptive behaviour is often now referred to as emotional behavioural difficulties or EBD. Although intuitively we all think we know what we mean by disruptive behaviour, formulating a precise definition can prove difficult. Before we go further it would be helpful to ask a few questions.

1 How would you define disruptive behaviour in fifty words or less?
2 How would you create a checklist designed to measure disruptive behaviour?
3 Did you find the above two questions easy, and why?

There have been many definitions put forward. Cooper defines EBD as:

> Any problem of an emotional or behavioural nature that is experienced by a young person to an extent that it interferes with their personal, social and/or educational development. . . . We take this to include psycho-social problems, such as socialised deviancy and delinquency; low self-esteem, anxiety, withdrawn and acting out behaviour. We also see it as falling under this broad heading problems of a broadly bio-psychosocial nature, such as those associated with ADHD, Autism and related conditions.
>
> (Cooper 1996, p. 1)

Charlton and David (1993) state that, from the school's point of view, EBD is seen as behaviour:

> which is manifested verbally or physically and which covertly challenges – to varying degrees and in a variety of ways – the authority of the teacher or the school.
>
> (cited in Daniels *et al.* 1999, p. 116)

It would seem that this definition implies that EBD is to some extent a social construction, in that the problem is not within the individual but is created through the individual's interaction in a certain social environment. Therefore the definition of EBD would very much depend on the interpretation of the individual teacher or the individual school. This is a key point.

Effects

Garner and Hill (1995) define disruptive behaviour in terms of its negative consequences or effects. Disruptive behaviour is:

> Behaviour which prevents children's participation in educational activities; isolates them from their peers; affects the learning and functioning of other pupils; drastically reduces their opportunities for involvement in ordinary community activities; makes excessive demands upon teachers, staff and resources; places the child or others in physical danger; and makes future placement difficult.
>
> (cited in Daniels *et al.* 1999, p. 118)

It is also essential that emotional and behavioural difficulties be distinguished from general naughtiness and transient emotional difficulties (Daniels *et al.* 1999).

How teachers define disruptive behaviour

There are numerous definitions, but what are we to make of all of this? Perhaps it would be helpful to ask how teachers would define disruptive behaviour or EBD. One school highlighted in the DfEE report *Emotional and Behavioural Difficulties in Mainstream Schools* (Daniels *et al.* 1999) had in place a 'pupil behavioural enquiry form'. On this form teachers were asked to rate the pupil's behaviour on a scale of 1 to 4 (1 = no cause for concern; 2 = mild cause for concern; 3 = moderate cause for concern, and 4 = serious cause for concern) in five areas (work skills, verbal behaviour, non-verbal behaviour, emotional profile and personal organisation). Some of the areas covered included:

- *Work skills*: presentation of work, care of own books and work, homework completion, settling to work, following verbal instructions, requesting help when appropriate, accepting guidance/advice.

- *Verbal behaviour*: refuses to follow instructions, talks when teacher is talking, talks to teacher instead of working, shouts out, mimics others, abuses/threatens other pupils, abuses/threatens teacher, makes inappropriate noises.
- *Non-verbal behaviour*: leaves classroom, wanders about classroom, fidgets in seat, engages in classroom horseplay, damages/takes other pupils' property.
- *Emotional profile*: easily reduced to tears, prone to outbursts of anger or tantrums, isolation from rest of group, physical self-abuse, cannot express feelings.
- *Personal organisation*: truants from lessons, truants from school, arrives late, leaves coat on, fails to bring books or equipment.

Of course what would constitute 'no cause for concern' and what would constitute 'serious cause for concern' would need to be discussed and agreed upon.

After looking at these varied definitions are we any closer to an understanding of what disruptive behaviour is? Perhaps the complexity apparent in the definitions is due to the fact that disruptive behaviour can take many forms and there are many types of disruptive behaviour. It would also seem from these varied definitions that there are multiple causes for such disruptive behaviour.

Who has EBD?

It is difficult to ascertain just how many students could be classified as having EBD. The Elton Committee (DES 1989) found no empirical evidence to suggest that behavioural difficulties were increasing in schools. Yet if we look at the statistics regarding school exclusions, which are presumably based on challenging behaviour, a different picture emerges. School exclusions increased from 2,910 in 1990/1991 to 12,000 in 1995/1996 (Parsons 1996). Statistics reveal that in 1997/1998 there were 12,298 students who were permanently excluded from schools in England; 84 per cent of the exclusions concerned boys. Ethnicity was a factor, with black Caribbean students having the highest exclusion rate, and Chinese students having the lowest rate. It was also noted that children who are looked after by the local authorities are ten times more likely to be excluded than any other students (ONS 2000).

Diagnosis

The first step in dealing with EBD is to have some system of identification, such as the 'pupil behavioural enquiry form' mentioned earlier. The DfEE report *Emotional and Behavioural Difficulties in Mainstream Schools* (Daniels *et al.* 1999) stated that appropriate assessment was problematic due in part to difficulties and confusions in regard to definitions. Once a pupil was identified as being at risk for EBD then the pupil needed to be put on the Special Needs Register and go through the necessary stages as outlined by the Code of Practice. (See Chapter 4.)

Explanations/causes/interventions

Many possible causes have been put forward. The Pack Report (SED 1977) outlined possible causes as being: early maturation, raising school-leaving age, unsettlement, dislike of secondary provision, teacher shortage, high staff turnover, and teachers who cannot cope. Ogilvy (1994) felt that causation could be attributed to three factors: those stemming from within the child, those stemming from the home/community, and those pertaining to the school. An interesting study (Reybekill 1998) asked pupils with EBD and teachers to give explanations for disruptive behaviour and truancy. Pupils with EBD felt that individual teachers and their teaching styles were the reason for their behaviour. Teachers on the other hand blamed the pupils, their families and their peers. Neither teachers nor pupils with EBD were willing to acknowledge their own role in the problem. Ogilvy (1994) argues that the difficulty with discussing causation is that this line of enquiry often seeks to find single explanations for the behaviour. These explanations can see the child, the home, or the school as being the cause. Ogilvy argues that such a linear explanation is not helpful, as it tends to simplify a very complex situation. An interactional or systemic approach is needed.

We could categorise the possible causes of disruptive behaviour as follows:

1 *Behavioural*: this view would argue that on some level the behaviour is being reinforced. Possibly the behaviour is initially learned through a process of observational learning, whereby an individual sees disruptive behaviour of another being reinforced.

2 *Psychodynamic*: this view would argue that there are unresolved conflicts possibly dating from early childhood which are underlying the behaviour.

3 *Bio-psychosocial*: this view would see the individual as having specific learning difficulties of a biological nature, such as ADHD or autism spectrum disorder. These conditions would result in the individual having difficulties in interacting in a social environment. Undiagnosed dyslexia could also cause some individuals to act out.

4 *Eco-system approach*: this view would argue that all individuals belong to a set of social sub-systems and that their behaviour is a result of interaction within and between these sub-systems.

5 Perhaps there is a complex interaction between some or all of the above.

What is important to note is that often the presumed cause/explanation will dictate the form of intervention. Sometimes a distinction is made between preventive and corrective measures. This distinction relates to timing. When do teachers become concerned regarding behaviour? When do they intervene? Before there is a problem (preventive), when the problem is just becoming apparent, or when they are in the middle of a crisis (corrective)? In the next section we will discuss in more detail possible causes and recommended interventions. It is also important to note that some of the interventions mentioned could be used as either preventive or corrective measures.

Progress exercise 8.1

Case study

Jamie is just 5 and is enrolled in a reception class at his local primary school. The teachers report that Jamie is uncontrollable. When asked to define what she meant by uncontrollable, Jamie's teacher stated:

Jamie cannot sit still; not even for ten seconds. He is constantly fidgeting. If he does not get to do what he wants to do he screams and screams and throws himself on the floor. These tantrums can last for twenty to thirty minutes at a time. He hits, kicks and bites the other children.

Questions

1 What types of disruptive behaviour is Jamie displaying?

2 What are the effects of Jamie's disruptive behaviour?

3 Would all aspects of Jamie's behaviour be considered disruptive in all environments?

Presumed causes: psychodynamic

This approach will argue that an individual's problems, in this instance EBD, are the result of their earliest experiences, specifically the relationship the individual has with its caregivers. Attachment theory focuses on the interaction between a child and its parent, or substitute caregiver. A young child will display proximity-seeking attachment behaviour in the form of emotionally charged demands for attention. These demands for attention can take the form of screams, tantrums or severely withdrawn behaviour. With appropriate childcare – that is, childcare that is neither neglectful nor over-protective – a child will be able to establish a sense of security and well-being. With a firm sense of well-being the child will have the confidence to explore its environment and move on to more socially accepted forms of communicating. Within this framework, a child with EBD is seen to have had difficulties with this early stage of development and consequently to have become stuck at or to have regressed to a point where their needs were last met satisfactorily (Tyrer and Steinberg 1993). The result is that, although the child grows up, they continue to exhibit behaviours and experience emotions from a much earlier stage of development. Of course their behaviour is deemed inappropriate in comparison to the developmentally appropriate behaviour exhibited by their peers (Cooper and Lovey 1999).

Psychodynamic interventions: nurture groups

The teacher faced with such a child has a number of options. In struggling to handle a difficult child the teacher could experience personal or professional failure and could blame either the child or themselves. What is needed is for the teacher to recognise that the child, for whatever reason, does not have the necessary skills and that therefore: 'the adults must meet them at the level they have reached and offer the structures, the level of control, the teaching and the emotional acceptance and encouragement necessary for the child to move on' (Bennathan 1997, p. 24).

Although this intervention is psychodynamic, the emphasis on meeting the child at their level and providing structures seems reminiscent of Vygotsky's concept of the Zone of Proximal Development and scaffolding.

One approach within this area is what is referred to as **nurture groups**. Nurture groups were first established by the ILEA (Inner London Education Authority) in the 1970s by Marjorie Boxall, an educational psychologist. The rationale behind nurture groups was based on attachment theory (Bowlby 1965). Bowlby stressed that the development of attachment bonds was important for later emotional health. Nurture groups are designed as an intervention for very young children, aged 4 or 5, coming into the educational system. The classes are located within mainstream schools. The child will be in a mainstream class for registration, after which the child will be taken to the group room. The room where the nurture group is held will in part resemble a classroom with desks, but it will also have a home atmosphere with sofas, cushions, curtains at the window and a separate kitchen and eating area. Nurture groups cater for 10 to 12 children at a time and the aim is that most children who are in a nurture group will be able to rejoin a mainstream classroom after one year.

Bennathan (1997) states that nurture groups are for children who, if the provision were not available, would be excluded from mainstream school and offered a special placement.

Nurture groups aim to be friendly places. There is a lot of structure, ritual and repetition. Rules are made clear and rules are rehearsed. Teachers, through their personal relationships with the child, hope to communicate that the child is valued and cared for. Opportunities for the whole group, or smaller groups, to meet several times a day are created, where the children are encouraged to share ideas not only in regard to schoolwork but also in terms of their behaviour. It is hoped that through such discussions a child will become aware of the meaning and consequences of their behaviour, realise that they have choices and begin to develop inner controls (Cooper and Lovey 1999).

Evaluation of nurture groups

It would seem that the need for the child to feel valued and cared for is central to this treatment. In a sense the teachers are trying to create a relationship with the child and, once the child knows that some adult values them, then they can move forward. However, how a person expresses warmth or acceptance, or to what degree, is difficult to measure. A teacher might think they are communicating a sense of worth and value to their student, but whether that is how the student experiences the teacher's responses is another issue.

Cooper and Lovey (1999) state that systematic studies evaluating the effectiveness of nurture groups are rare. However, one recent study carried out by the London Borough of Enfield (Iszatt and Wasilewska 1997) recorded the progress of 308 children who had been placed in nurture groups since the 1980s: 86 per cent of the children after spending less than a year in a nurture group were able to successfully integrate back into a mainstream class; 83 per cent of these children required no further special educational need support. This was compared to a group of twenty children, who were similar to the children who had been placed in nurture groups, but for whom no nurture group placement could be found: 35 per cent of these children ended up in special schools, with 55 per cent managing to cope in mainstream schools without support.

Although the above examples of nurture groups involve young children, pyschodynamic therapies are available for individuals of any age. However, as Greenhalgh (1994) argues, most of these interventions are of a medium- to long-term nature and therefore inappropriate for the average classroom teacher. In addition, pyschodynamic therapy needs to be conducted by a suitably qualified individual.

Presumed causes: bio-psychosocial

This approach would argue that the individual's disruptive behaviour is a result of an underlying physiological or biological condition. A diagnosis of such a condition would call for specific medical interventions. Barkley (1998) argues that ADHD results from a failure in self-control due to key brain circuits that fail to develop properly. Barkley (1998) further speculates that this failure in development stems from altered genes. La Hoste *et al.* (1996) discovered that a variant of the dopamine receptor gene D4 is more prevalent in children with ADHD. With the advent of brain imaging devices, certain brain regions have been implicated in this condition.

When looking at the diagnostic criteria of ADHD there are many criteria that could be interpreted as disruptive behaviour within the classroom. In a sense, with ADHD, professionals are not only concerned with the disruptive and impulsive behaviour that marks the condition, but also with the negative secondary effects that could occur if a diagnosis is not made. If a child cannot sustain attention, cannot control their impulses, the child will find it difficult to succeed academically at school. Lack of academic success could lead to poor self-esteem, to the child being labelled as disruptive and lazy, and possibly to more disruptive behaviour. A lack of impulse control could lead an individual to be at greater risk of making poor choices in regard to engaging in anti-social behaviour.

Bio-psychosocial interventions

Interventions for ADHD have often taken the form of psycho-stimulants, the most widely prescribed being Ritalin. Psychostimulants have been found to improve the behaviour of between 70 and 90 per cent of children with ADHD. This reported improvement often takes the form of the children being less impulsive, less prone to distraction and less restless. This would certainly mean that these children would be seen as less disruptive within a classroom environment. Further, psychostimulants have been reported to enable children to hold more information in their mind, to become more academically productive and to gain better self-control (Barkley 1998).

Evaluation of Ritalin

However, the use of psychostimulants is not without its critics or criticisms. There is controversy concerning the diagnosis of ADHD. Certainly the behavioural consequences of this condition could have other explanations. Family difficulties and emotional problems could cause problems with inattention, hyperactivity and impulsivity. Critics will say that diagnosis of ADHD is extremely difficult, and a wrong diagnosis will mean that children will unnecessarily be prescribed psychostimulants.

Even those who proclaim the effectiveness of Ritalin caution that its usage needs to be monitored. Ritalin is a short-acting medication, in that the drug does not build up significantly in the bloodstream. As Ritalin is a short-acting medication multiple doses need to be given. Ritalin begins to work in 20–40 minutes, with maximum effectiveness occurring after one and a half hours, and the effects wearing off in about four hours. The correct timing and dosage for each child need to be determined and constantly reviewed. If the child seems over-sedated, the dosage is too high. In some children an effect known as rebound hyperactivity can occur. What this means is that, as the dosage wears off, the child becomes increasingly hyperactive, in fact more hyper-active than they were before commencing medication. An infrequent long-term side-effect of Ritalin is the gradual emergence of paranoia. This occurs in approximately 2 per cent of individuals taking Ritalin and usually the symptoms occur when the individual is entering adolescence.

Critics have talked about psychological dependency and the issue of how an individual makes sense of the fact that they need to take a drug to control their behaviour. Whalen and Henker (1991) argue that the individual might interpret their usage of medication as a reflection of a continuous need for chemical assistance in order to sustain personal competence and control, and that this in turn could have a negative effect on them developing a sense of self as agent. However, others will argue that medication is extremely beneficial in that it provides a window of opportunity, allowing the individual to make progress academically and to control impulsive responses, and thus reducing the risk that the individual will make the wrong choices.

In summary, even the most enthusiastic supporters of the use of Ritalin will affirm that medication is not enough and advocate a multi-disciplinary approach. (See Chapter 9 for information on the ADHD classroom.)

Presumed causes: behavioural

This view sees challenging behaviour as the result of a vicious circle whereby:

- The child presents difficult behaviour, i.e. the child hits another child in class.
- The adult responds with punitive behaviour, i.e. tells the child that he is a useless vicious thug and sends him out of the class.
- The child gains attention and feels rewarded on the basis that any attention is better than no attention.
- The child becomes the baddie.
- This leads to more difficult behaviour.

This cycle needs to be broken by paying lots of attention to the child when the child is behaving well.

Behaviourist interventions and evaluation

The most favoured strategy used by teachers to improve behaviour seems to be to pay positive attention to pupils when they are behaving well (Daniels *et al.* 1999), that is, 'catching them being good'. This is all very much a reworking of Skinner's ideas in regard to behaviour modification, with an emphasis on reinforcement. In terms of the use of rewards it has been found that the rewards need to be negotiated with the pupils so that they are truly seen as rewarding. Rewards might be in the form of vouchers for shops or burgers. Rewards must be earned. They must relate to clear and agreed targets. There must be fairness in the system (Daniels *et al.* 1999).

What teachers do not want is comments from students such as:

'I can remember being in Year 8. I worked really hard. I always handed in my work on time. There were these two other students in the class and they were always getting more merits than I did. It seemed like they would earn a merit just for turning up or for swearing in the lesson only once. If other students swore in the lesson we were down for detention. It just wasn't fair.'

The above example illustrates a very difficult issue, which can be summarised as the conflict of the needs of the individual versus the need to be fair to all (Daniels *et al.* 1999). Sometimes in dealing with pupils with EBD minor misdemeanours are purposely ignored by teachers, but when this does occur it is suggested that other classmates are made aware of the reasons for this strategy. Evidence suggests that with such discussion other students can be understanding and tolerant (Daniels *et al.* 1999).

Behavioural techniques are one effective way of dealing with disruptive behaviour but consideration needs to focus on how they are applied. It is suggested that the interventions are carefully monitored, and that these behaviourist approaches are accompanied by humanistic or psychodynamic interventions which involve listening and talking with the pupil (Daniels *et al.* 1999). The key point is that behaviourist interventions will not work on all students at all times. They need to be used in conjunction with other approaches.

Eco-systems approaches

Eco-systems approaches argue that all children or all individuals belong to a set of social sub-systems and that their behaviour is a result of interactions within and between these sub-systems.

Certainly it has been argued that the first step in dealing with EBD is to recognise that 'disruption is a school-generated problem' (McGuiness and Craggs 1986). It has been argued (Molnar and Lindquist 1989) that teachers and institutions help to maintain the problem of disruptive behaviour by their frozen perceptions of a student in terms of their past behaviour. What is needed is that they acknowledge a mismatch between sub-systems, and re-frame the behaviour, thus removing blame and avoiding conflict. For example, if a student is verbally abusive to a teacher, the teacher needs to re-frame the problem. This approach does not mean that the teacher has to pretend that the student has not been verbally abusive, but the teacher needs to cognitively re-frame the situation. The teacher needs to think beyond what has just taken place as being a result of the student being bad, or of them being an ineffective teacher. The student's behaviour needs to be seen as the system of the school not being able to cope with this particular student, or the student not being able to cope with the school system. Therefore it is the interaction between the school system and the needs of the individual that needs to be looked at.

Disruptive behaviour: ways forward

This chapter has frequently alluded to the Daniels *et al.* (1999) research report on *Emotional and Behavioural Difficulties in Mainstream Schools*. The aim of this report was to identify how mainstream schools achieved effective practice in the assessment of and provision for pupils with EBD. Schools identified as having good practice in regard to EBD were visited and ten such schools were studied in depth. In summary, it was found that the following characteristics underlie success in addressing the needs of children with EBD:

- Good teaching: factors mentioned included matching teaching to learning style, having high expectations, motivating students, offering support sensitively.
- An appropriate curriculum that the students can access.

- An effective behaviour policy: policies were written, policies were known, and there was an emphasis on living the policies.
- Staff who are able to learn from their actions. Staff were encouraged to discuss concerns, to share ideas, to reflect on instances where things went wrong, to learn from previous situations, and to develop effective practices.
- Key staff who understand the nature of emotional and behavioural difficulties.

Summary

Disruptive behaviour or emotional behavioural difficulties is an area of current concern and continuing research. Good working definitions and effective means of diagnosis are needed. It would seem that there are many types of disruptive behaviour. This chapter has looked at the relationship between effects, causes/explanations and intervention strategies. Although two students might exhibit the same disruptive behaviour, the behaviour might be interpreted differently depending on definitions of what constitutes disruptive behaviour. Similarly, the two students, although exhibiting the same behaviour, might engage in the behaviour for different reasons. The cause, or explanation, for the behaviour often determines the intervention. But as any one disruptive behaviour could have several different causes, suitable interventions might utilise a number of possible approaches.

Review exercise

1 With reference to the case study of Jamie mentioned earlier in this chapter (see p. 140), outline possible causes for his behaviour and appropriate intervention strategies.

2 Of the interventions mentioned in this chapter, which could be used as preventive measures and which could be used as corrective measures?

Further reading

Daniels, H., Visser, J., Cole, T. and Reybekill, N. de (1999) *Emotional and Behavioural Difficulties in Mainstream Schools*, School of Education, University of Birmingham, DfEE, RR90. A very long comprehensive report, but well worth reading.

Journals such as *Emotional and Behavioural Difficulties* provide a valuable source of information.

9

Design and layout of educational environments

Introduction

It is helpful to begin by bringing to mind various images of classrooms and schools you have known. For example, what can you remember of your first days at a new school? You of course will remember the other students, the teacher perhaps, but what of the room and the school itself? Were you overwhelmed by the size of the building? Did you get lost in the corridors? Did you have your own desk? Did you feel hemmed in by the sheer numbers of other students? Did you feel that there were certain environments that were more conducive to effective learning? Can any environment be conducive to learning, you ask? Let me give you an example. Imagine you have enrolled on a college course on ancient Babylonian culture with an eminent professor. The class is scheduled for every Tuesday, just after lunch. The room is small, hot and has no windows. The lecture consists of the professor turning off the lights and showing slides of his latest visit to the museum in Baghdad. The question is how much learning will take place under these conditions? This chapter will look at various aspects of the environment, and their impact on performance and feelings, and at means of creating better environments for learning.

Environmental psychology

Simply put, environmental psychology studies the relationship between behaviour and the environment in which the behaviour occurs. Environment, in this context, is taken to mean the physical environment – for example, noise, light, crowding, temperature – and the ways in which architects design working space. Early research in this field tended to study individual reactions to environmental stimuli – for example, the effects of light or noise – in controlled laboratory conditions. However, there were difficulties in generalising such research to real life environments. Later research tended to look at the environmental context. Environmental determinism emphasises the environmental effects on behaviour but fails to acknowledge the inter-relationship between the two. In its most extreme form what is known as 'architectural determinism' states that people can adapt to any arrangement of space and that behaviour in a given environment is caused entirely by the characteristics of the environment (Corsini and Auerbach 1996, p. 303). However, common sense would tell us otherwise. Certainly some environmental situations constrain behaviour. There is only so much you can do in a lift. Some environmental situations offer options. In a supermarket you have a choice of what aisles to go down and in what order. Environment is not all, as we learn what is deemed to be socially appropriate behaviour in certain environments. Personality is also a key factor within this debate. Different people can have completely different reactions to the same environment. Some individuals will struggle against their environment, in order to change it. Nowadays most theorists would see the relationship between behaviour and environment as complex.

Physical features of the learning environment

It is suggested that schools should provide students with a variety of teaching spaces, including classrooms and rooms for smaller groups. There should be opportunities and space provided for PE, music and drama (DfE 1992). Moyles (1992, p. 6) lists key physical features of the learning environment (see Table 9.1).

Table 9.1 Physical features of the learning environment

Class Base	Resources	Outside area
• Physical area (how big is the classroom?) • Use of space and its impact on movement (seating arrangements, small groups vs. rows) • Furniture/furnishings (i.e. tables, desks, chairs, shelving units, play equipment, etc.) • Sound: acoustics • Lighting • Heat • Visual impact (created by décor and displays, etc.) • Safety constraints	• Other people (i.e. classroom assistants) • Presentation of materials and displays • Accessibility of resources and materials	• Corridors • Library • Resource centre • Outside environment (wildlife areas, playgrounds)

The aim for the teacher is to organise his/her environment such that effective learning takes place. The general appearance of the classroom indicates to pupils the care that goes into their learning (Kyriacou 1991). The arrangement of the classroom should enable the students to learn more quickly and effectively, and promote learning that is enjoyable (Bull and Solity 1987).

In the next section we will consider several features of the learning environment and their effects on performance and feelings.

Effects of physical features on performance and feelings

Use of physical area: seating arrangements

Table 9.2 looks at the advantages and disadvantages of four possible seating arrangements. The next question concerns whether one seating arrangement is superior to another.

Table 9.2 Types of seating arrangements: advantages and disadvantages

Seating arrangement	Advantages	Disadvantages
Desks are placed in rows	• Discourages non-productive talk. • Encourages the student to focus on required task. • Suitable for whole group instruction, i.e. lectures, and individual work.	• Arrangement makes group work and discussions difficult. • Some students will be closer to the blackboard than others. • Possible disadvantage for those who sit at the back.
Semicircle	• Teacher can see all students. • Students can see each other, the teacher and the blackboard. • Lends itself to classroom discussions, group work and even lectures.	• Some concern that this approach would make classroom control more difficult. • Some concern that there would be problems with background noise (talking).
Clusters of desks in groups of four or five	• Conducive to group work. • Easy to share resources and materials.	• Some may have difficulty seeing the board. • Concern with background noise.
Activity zones/learning bays – different stations in classroom for each subject, i.e. history, maths, science and reading	• Conducive to group work centred around activity.	• Individual would not have their own desk. • Concern with background noise. • Difficult for whole group teaching.

Getzels (1974) noted higher levels of activity in classrooms with activity zones than in classrooms with seats arranged in rows. However Getzels (1974) advocated no specific seating arrangement as seating arrangements would need to reflect the particular learning needs of the students, the subject matter to be taught and the instructional strategy to be used. Activity zones are particularly relevant to the primary school child. Wilkinson (1988) states that learning bays, or activity zones, permit maximum use of the outside edges of a room, allowing more movement in the middle. Nash (1981) and Field (1988) state that the complexity of activities, the commitment to these activities and concentration on task are increased when classrooms are split into learning bays/activity zones. However Moyles (1992) states that there needs to be a balance between whole class teaching and learning bays: the learning bays need to be partitioned in such a manner that all students can still focus on the teacher. Cullingford (1991) states that students prefer to have their own particular part of the classroom, their own desk, and their own view. Having your own space creates a feeling of ownership.

Although desks arranged in groups or clusters lend themselves to students being involved in group work, what activities do students in such seating arrangements participate in?

Gavienas (1999) conducted a study to investigate the reasons behind how primary teachers arrange their classrooms for group teaching. This was a small study carried out in one school with eleven classrooms. The teachers observed used a group teaching method. This method involved students being seated in small groups or clusters. The teachers would move around the various groups. While the teacher was involved in direct teaching with one group, the other groups would be given a follow-up task. Fifty-three out of seventy-two follow-up tasks observed were written tasks. Sixty-six out of the seventy-two follow-up tasks observed were expected to be undertaken individually. Although the students were in groups the expectation was that students would not talk to each other but that they would get on with the task at hand. During follow-up interviews the teachers commented that the seating arrangement was not due to any educational theory, but that it was due to practical considerations. It was easier to organise resources when students were seated in groups, and the continuous flat surface of the grouped desks or tables made it easier for the students to share resources. This study confirms the findings of Galton and Williamson (1992), who found that although students were seated in ability groups

50 per cent of the time, they were only expected to work as a group 5 per cent of the time. Gavienas concludes that:

> [the] practice of seating children in social groups, but requiring them to work individually may be counter productive. If we persist in seating children together in social groups, but try to prevent them from talking to each other, we might be creating new tensions.
>
> (Gavienas 1999, p. 2)

Resources

Nash (1981) states that students will use resources more effectively if the resources are organised in a logical fashion and they are near at hand. The teacher needs to explain the organisational system to the students and encourage them to use the resources. This encouragement engenders ownership. It communicates to the students that the classroom and resources are their learning environment, and in this way the students feel empowered (Moyles 1992).

Sound/acoustics

Fifty-four per cent of classroom teachers and 77 per cent of PE teachers surveyed stated that noise caused communication problems most of the time (Edwards 1997). In terms of sound, the average volume of a teacher's voice in the classroom is 65–70 dBA. The typical classroom has a background noise level ranging from 55 to 75 dBA. So it would seem that a teacher's voice is often only equal in volume to the background noise. It is not surprising then that teachers complain that they have difficulties in making themselves heard. Edwards (1997) states that many groups of children would have difficulties in understanding speech in a classroom with background noise levels of 65–70 dBA. These include:

- young children with normal hearing
- children who are non-native English speakers
- children with articulation problems
- individuals with language learning disorders and/or listening difficulties
- individuals with minimal hearing loss or recurring ear infections

Maxwell and Evans (2000), summarising the effects that noise has on young children, state that research has centred on motivational effects and cognitive effects, including: memory, attention and academic achievement. In terms of academic achievement Evans and Maxwell (1997) found a link between chronic noise exposure and reading. They compared children's reading skills in two schools. The 'noisy school' was near an airport, with planes flying over the school approximately every six minutes. The decibel level in the classroom was in the nineties. Children from both schools were tested for reading skills under quiet conditions. The children in the 'noisy school' had poorer reading skills than the children in the 'quieter school'. Evans and Maxwell (1997) speculate that language skills are related to reading skills and that noise is related to both. Possibly excessive noise interferes with the ability to discriminate between general noise and meaningful auditory information. In this sense young children exposed to excessive noise will have difficulties in acquiring and understanding speech and this will affect academic performance. To investigate this further, Maxwell and Evans (2000) studied pre-reading skills in 4-year-old children who were attending a day-care centre. The day-care centre was excessively noisy (peak 96.8–99.1 dBA, average 75.8–77.1 dBA). The management of the centre, recognising that this was an issue, took steps to remedy the situation by the installation of sound-absorbent panels. After renovation the day-care centre was less noisy (peak 87.2–95.2 dBA, average 69.4–73.9 dBA). Pre-reading skills were measured for all children before and after renovation, in quiet conditions. Children achieved higher scores after renovation.

> Children were rated by their classroom teacher as having better language skills (e.g. child speaks well enough to be understood by others, child uses sentences, not just words) and the children performed better on a cognitive language skill measure.
>
> (Maxwell and Evans 2000, p. 3)

Lighting

Good quality lighting is conducive to effective teaching. Neill (1991) notes that the teacher, when talking, should not be in the shadows, as very young children rely on facial expressions and body language to give them clues to the meaning of language. The quality of lighting is crucial for visually impaired students who might have some useful residual vision. For these individuals the visual environment can either aid or hinder their learning. It is suggested that an environmental audit be carried out to look for such problems as glare created by light reflecting off walls and surfaces. In order to enhance the quality of the visual environment the key is to provide contrast and clarity. For example, if visually impaired students can differentiate between the door handle and the door then they can leave or enter the room unaided, thus fostering independence (Ackerly and Lomas 1998).

Class size

Much has been written on class size. Research (Nfer Press Release 1998) has reported that large classes (over thirty students) undermine teachers' morale and adversely affect the quality of teaching received by the students. Headteachers reported that although good teachers could teach large classes, it was usually at the expense of the teachers' own well-being in terms of decreased motivation, self-esteem and morale. The teachers reported that large classes resulted in more time being spent on management of activities and less time being spent with individual children. Although teachers managed to cover and assess all aspects of the National Curriculum, they reported that they rarely felt fully satisfied with what they had achieved. Teachers felt that over-crowded classrooms had negative effects on student behaviour and learning.

Johnson and Jamison (1998) state that reports from the government's school inspectorate suggest that there are some benefits for children when class sizes are reduced. These benefits are more likely to apply to children in Key Stage 1 (ages 5–7). However, while acknowledging the benefits of smaller classes, the quality of teaching is a more important factor in determining effective learning than is class size.

Table 9.3 A summary of teachers' views on class size

Larger classes	Smaller classes
• Pupils receive less individual attention.	• Pupils receive more individual attention.
• A more restricted range of teaching and learning activities on offer.	• More varied learning and teaching styles possible.
• Whole class teaching is sometimes used for control and to keep students on task.	• Whole class teaching methods only used when appropriate for the activity.
• Group work not viable due to too many groups or the groups being too large.	• Group work becomes more manageable and an effective teaching strategy.
• Restricted opportunities for individual assessment and feedback.	• More time for individual assessment and feedback.
• Limitations on practical activities that can be carried out.	• More reasonable workload for teachers which enables the teachers to focus their energy on meeting the educational needs of their students.

Imagine that you are teaching a Year 1 class with twenty-nine children. You have one large rectangular room with a large white board against one wall, two windows on another wall, and one large storage cupboard placed against another wall. How will you design your ideal classroom environment? Justify your recommendations in terms of beneficial impact on performance or feelings.

Progress exercise 9.1

Creating better environmental conditions for learning

As we stated earlier, how you design your environment depends very much on who you are teaching, what you are teaching and how you are teaching. In the next section we will look at applications of research into the relationship between environment and behaviour where specific environments are seen to enhance learning for distinct groups of students.

The ADHD classroom

Detweiler and colleagues (1995) reported on what they term 'the ADHD classroom', a classroom specifically adapted for pupils with ADHD. 'The ideal ADHD classroom combines the seemingly contra-dictory attributes of consistency and flexibility, a consistent predictable setting which provides much structure, limited distraction and flexibility in addressing each student's individual learning style' (Detweiler *et al*. 1995, p. 5). Such classrooms would have the following characteristics:

- Small class sizes – ten or fewer children – with a teacher and one support assistant.
- A room with four walls and no open space leading into other classrooms.
- No changing of teachers. Subjects always taught in the same order.
- Soundproofing of rooms. Few distractions.
- Daily individualised programmes and weekly schedules on each desk for easy access.
- Separate study booths, or offices, for each child.
- A 'time out' room near by.
- A fan in each study booth, to be used by students to block out extraneous noise.

These techniques have been derived from work with thousands of children with ADHD (Detweiler *et al*. 1995). Possibly such a classroom design is effective in that it minimises external distractions and helps the student to focus on the task at hand.

Multi-sensory rooms

Multi-sensory rooms offer a range of experiences involving sight, sound, touch and smell, and are particularly suitable for students with complex physical, sensory and learning needs (DfE 1992). These rooms can be used for relaxation as well as education. A white room is designed for deep relaxation and offers soothing lights and comfortable music. A dark room can offer those visually impaired students with some useful residual vision a chance to react to visual stimuli in a dark environment where the contrast is at its greatest and the visual stimuli can be controlled (Gerald 1998). Often dark rooms are equipped with state-of-the-art technology in terms of sound and light. The key factor is that these light and sound effects are controlled by switches which students with complex needs can be taught how to use, thus giving the student a sense of control over their environment. The use of such multi-sensory rooms can be linked to National Curriculum assessments such as Key Stage 1, Programme of Study: 'Controlling and Modelling: recognise that controls are integral to many everyday devices' (Shaw 1998).

Environmental implications for autistic students

With inclusion of children with special educational needs within main-stream schools on the government's agenda (DfEE 1997: *Excellence for All Children*), consideration needs to be given to differential needs of specific groups of students. Some individuals with autism will have IQs within the normal range, but being autistic they will have a different way of 'being' (Preston 1998). One difficulty that some individuals with high-functioning autism talk about is distortions in sensory perception. Temple Grandin is an assistant professor at Colorado State University and describes herself as autistic. She writes of distortions in sensory perception which can make learning within a classroom environment problematic: 'When I was a child, loud sounds like the school bell hurt my ears like a dentist drill hitting a nerve' (Grandin 1998, p. 2). Preston (1998) notes that while some autistic individuals respond with fear to sounds such as the tearing of a piece of paper, they might seem to not hear or ignore sounds such as a huge clap of thunder, which frighten other children. Grandin (1998) further comments that some autistic individuals are sensitive to visual distractions and fluorescent lights: 'They can see the flicker of the 60 cycle electricity' (Grandin 1998, p. 2). Preston (1998) comments that teachers need to consider this sensory sensitivity. Grandin (1998) has her own suggestions. Bells could be tolerated if muffled slightly by stuffing the bell with tissue. The sound of scraping chairs, which can be experienced as painful, could be silenced by placing a slit tennis ball on the leg-ends or by laying down a carpet. Light bulbs should be replaced before they wear out, as newer bulbs flicker less.

Summary

This chapter has looked at numerous physical features of educational environments, including the use of space (how many students, where and how to place students) and sensory concerns (sound and lighting). Without a doubt physical features have an impact on performance and feelings. This chapter has highlighted the concepts of ownership and empowerment. In attempting to design an ideal learning environment it is necessary to consider who you are teaching, what you are teaching and the teaching and learning styles that you want to use.

Review exercise

To what extent do the design and layout of an educational environment depend on who you are teaching?

Further reading

Moyles, J.R. (1992) *Organizing for Learning in the Primary Classroom*, Buckingham: Open University Press. A very interesting and practical book aimed at teachers.

Leadbetter, J. *et al.* (1999) *Applying Psychology in the Classroom*, London: David Fulton. This book has an interesting chapter on 'Understanding the Learning Environment'.

Gifford, R. (1987) *Environmental Psychology*, London: Allyn and Bacon. This book has a very informative and comprehensive chapter on 'Learning and the Physical Environment'.

10

Study aids

IMPROVING YOUR ESSAY WRITING SKILLS

At this point in the book you have acquired the knowledge necessary to tackle the exam itself. Answering exam questions is a skill which this chapter shows you how to improve. Examiners obviously have firsthand knowledge about what goes wrong in exams. For example, candidates frequently do not answer the question that has been set, but instead answer the one that they hoped would come up; or they do not make effective use of the knowledge they have but just 'dump their psychology' on the page and hope the examiner will sort it out for them. A grade 'C' answer usually contains appropriate material but tends to be limited in detail and commentary. To lift such an answer to a grade 'A' or 'B' may require no more than a little more detail, better use of material and coherent organization. It is important to appreciate that it may not involve writing at any greater length, but might even necessitate the elimination of passages that do not add to the quality of the answer and some elaboration of those that do.

By studying the essays presented in this chapter and the examiner's comments, you can learn how to turn your grade 'C' answer into a grade 'A'. Typically it only involves an extra 6 marks out of 30. Please note that marks given by the examiner in the practice essays should be used as a guide only and are not definitive.

You must provide the information that the examiner wants and not waste your time on irrelevant material. The answer will be marked out of 34 for the OCR exam board A level. Remember that these are the raw marks and not equivalent to those given on the examination certificate received ultimately by the candidate, because all examining boards are required to use a common standardized system, the Uniform Mark Scale (UMS), which adjusts all raw scores to a single standard across all boards. The questions from OCR are 'parted', that is, divided into sections. It is important to read the question (this is not as obvious as it sounds). Each section will have a set number of marks. This is an indication of the amount of material required and you must pace your answer accordingly. If a section carries 10 marks then it requires more material than one that carries 6.

The essays given here are notionally written by an 18-year-old in 30–40 minutes and they are marked bearing that in mind. By studying them you should be able to tell the difference between an average and a good essay. It is important when writing to such a tight time limit that you make every sentence count. It is likely that the first section will require you to demonstrate what you have learned about the topic being examined, and most students have acquired this type of skill at GCSE. Later sections will ask you to analyse and evaluate the material in the first section and apply your knowledge to a practical situation. This is a more difficult skill to master and will come with practice. Each essay in this chapter is followed by detailed comments about its strengths and weaknesses. The most common problems to watch out for are:

- Failing to answer the question but reproducing a model answer to a similar question which you have pre-learned.
- Not delivering the right balance between description and evaluation/ analysis. Remember that, for essay questions in this module, marking schemes are weighted 40 per cent towards knowledge and understanding and 60 per cent towards analysis and evaluation.
- Writing 'everything you know' about a topic in the hope that something will get credit and the examiner will sort your work out for you. Remember that excellence demands selectivity, so improvements can often be made by removing material that is irrelevant to the question set and elaborating material that *is* relevant.
- Failing to use your material effectively. It is not enough to place the information on the page – you must also show the examiner that you are using it to make a particular point.

Practice essay 1

(a) Outline the humanistic approach to education. (6 marks)

(b) Compare and contrast the humanistic approach with other explanations of education. (10 marks)

(OCR website 2001)

(a)

The humanistic approach is a person-centred, 'touchy feely' approach. It emphasises the role of the individual and a feel-good factor. A key person in the field is Rogers. Rogers stated that anything that could be taught was inconsequential and that real learning had to be self-discovered. Of course this would have applications for the teacher. If they don't teach what do they do? What are the taxpayers paying them for if not to teach?

Examiner's comments: Personal opinions on Rogers are not required in this part of the answer.

However, what Rogers meant was that the teacher takes a different role. The teacher would be a facilitator. The teacher would present learning resources and opportunities and ask questions. The teacher would also be seen as very much a learner in his own right. This approach would stress a positive relationship between student and teacher.

Examiner's comments: These are key points, which the candidate needs to expand on. For example, the candidate could outline Rogers' views in regard to teaching style and teaching environment as well as the relationship between teacher and student. Alternatively the candidate could outline the distinctions between humanistic content curricula, process curricula and school and group structures.

Maslow was another humanistic psychologist who believed that we all aimed for self-actualisation.

Examiner's comments: The candidate needs to say more in regard to how self-actualisation relates to education.

Two examples of humanistic approaches are co-operative learning techniques and emotional literacy classes.

Examiner's comments: Again this is a key point. A description of these approaches is needed. The candidate's answer on the whole is focused on the question and is mainly accurate and shows some evidence of elaboration. But the answer is too brief to gain full marks. The marks awarded for this section are 4/6.

(b)
The humanistic view of the teacher as a facilitator is somewhat reminiscent of Piaget and Bruner who advocate discovery learning.

Examiner's comments: This is a good point. But the candidate needs to expand on this point. It could be argued that Piaget with his emphasis on the importance of the processes of assimilation and accommodation in cognitive development places responsibility on the teacher for engineering opportunities where such processes could occur.

However Piaget and Bruner, as essentially cognitive development psychologists, stress the role of the thinking process in education, whereas Rogers is more concerned with the affective, feeling bit of individuality. I suppose the question is, how does affect (feeling) interact with thought processes and how do these factors interact within a classroom environment?

Examiner's comments: This is a key evaluative point. The candidate at this point could have mentioned the goals of collaborative learning, the role of motivation or attribution in education.

Pavlov talked about classical conditioning and said something about conditioned emotional responses.

Examiner's comments: Yes he did. An example would be beneficial at this point.

Skinner's approach to educational achievement was to see educational achievement as a function of environmental contingencies. Students work to receive praise and rewards. Though Skinner focused on observable aspects of behaviour, the concept of reinforcement can certainly be related to affect.

It would seem that to explain education a number of approaches are needed and those psychologists should concentrate on how all these approaches interact.

Examiner's comments: The candidate presents an overview of theories and makes some valid points in regard to comparing and contrasting. However, again the answer is too brief. This part of the question earns 5/10 marks, with the combined mark being 9/16, equivalent to a grade D.

Question 2

(a) **Describe what psychologists have discovered about the design and layout of classroom environments. (10 marks)**
(b) **Evaluate what psychologists have discovered about the design and layout of classroom environments. (16 marks)**
(c) **Giving reasons for your answers, suggest a number of design features a perfect classroom would have to maximise educational performance. (8 marks)**

(OCR website 2001)

(a)
Psychologists have been very interested in classroom design. Children spend a good 5 hours a day in the classroom for a good 10 months of the year. For children, time spent in the classroom seems like an eternity. What can psychologists and teachers do to the environment to make learning a pleasurable experience?

Examiner's comments: The candidate needs to make the connection between environmental layout and design and their effect on performance and feelings more explicit.

Bull and Solity (1987) state that the arrangement of the classroom should promote effective and enjoyable learning. To this end many psychologists have talked about a variety of seating arrangements. Seating arrangements could include such options as: the traditional set-up of desks in rows, desks placed in a semicircle, desks in groups or activity zones. Each of these seating arrangements has advantages and disadvantages. The advantages of desks being placed in rows are that it discourages students from talking to each other and encourages them to focus on the object at hand. This seating arrangement favours whole group teaching methods. The advantages of grouping students in a semicircle are that it is conducive to classroom discussions. The advantage of desks in groups is that it is conducive to group work and to sharing resources. Activity zones have been found to be very useful in infant schools.

Examiner's comments: The discussion is too general. The candidate could link such comments regarding seating design to specific studies. For example, in regard to activity zones or investigative bays, the candidate could have stated: 'Nash (1981) and Field (1988) found that activity zones in primary schools were associated with greater complexity in activity, greater commitment from individual students in regard to activities and greater levels of concentration.' Perhaps the candidate could make the connection between seating arrangements and noise and then discuss the various studies that have looked at the effect of noise on academic performance.

Lighting is an important variable. In a school for visually impaired children an environmental audit was conducted. Some visually impaired children have what is termed useful residual vision. Therefore appropriate lighting can enhance the learning process. On a similar tack, a psychologist could have an environmental audit in regard to hearing-impaired children who have useful residual hearing. This research seems to indicate that an individual approach is taken.

Examiner's comments: Good point, but reference to a specific study would help.

Class size is also an important consideration. Research regarding class size seems to indicate that infant class sizes over 30 lead to decreased motivation and self-esteem in teachers and more disruptive behaviour and less learning in students.

Examiner's comments: The candidate could have expanded on this point as there is much that could have been said. This section earns 6/10 marks.

(b)

While many psychologists have written on design and layout, there is a need to evaluate such findings. The research into advantages and disadvantages regarding classroom seating design is a case in point. If all seating arrangements have various advantages and disadvantages how does a teacher choose what type of seating arrangement to use? The first point to make is that it is important to consider who you are teaching, what you are teaching and what methods you are using. Getzels (1974) advocated that seating arrangements needed to reflect the particular learning needs of the students, the subject matter to be taught and the instructional strategy to be used. Field and Nash recommended the use of activity zones in primary schools. While this arrangement might benefit most primary students, individual differences need to be taken into account. The research regarding the educational needs of children with ADHD is a case in point. These students according to Detweiler *et al.* (1995) would benefit from a more structured environment. In fact Detweiler advocated individual study booths, which would not be available in your average primary school classroom, but perhaps sitting in desks in rows would help. However this raises the issue of balancing the special educational need of the few with the educational needs of the many.

Examiner's comments: Some very good evaluation here.

Early research tended to look at factors in isolation. What is needed is to look at factors in combination in real-life environments. Environmental or architectural determinism states that the environment causes/controls an individual's behaviour. But this position seems to ignore the individuality of individuals. For example, going back to our previous example you might find some research that says placing children in groups enhances educational performance, but what if the student had ADHD? Here the research would seem to indicate the exact opposite, that a more structured formal approach is needed. It would seem that future research into environmental design needs to take an individualistic approach.

Examiner's comments: Some key evaluative points, but somewhat repetitive. The candidate could have improved their mark by evaluating some other areas of research in this field (research on noise levels).

On the whole, the candidate mentions a few good points and presents a reasonably well-structured argument, and therefore this section is awarded 8/16 marks.

(c)

My ideal classroom concerns children in reception. In this classroom there are two students who have slight problems with vision.

Examiner's comments: It is a good idea to specify what group you are working with, as the group will determine the ideal characteristics.

Children will be placed in groups in investigative bays, building on the work of Nash and Field (mentioned earlier), but in such a way that they can all see the teacher.

The whole room will be carpeted to reduce background noise. This builds on the work of Edwards (1997) and Maxwell and Evans (2000).

Examiner's comments. While the candidate has mentioned the work of Nash and Field previously, the candidate has not mentioned the work of Edwards (1997) or Maxwell and Evans (2000). The candidate needs not only to briefly mention what their work was, but also why it provides a rationale for having the floor carpeted.

A carpeted space will be provided for the children to come to the front and sit and listen to the teacher. Care will be taken to ensure adequate lighting, again building on the work of Neill (1991).

Examiner's comments: Again what did Neill (1991) say, and how does lighting enhance academic achievement?

Care will be taken to ensure that the room is bright and cheery. Displays will be carefully set out. Class size will be 20 children to one teacher and two teaching assistants.

Examiner's comments: The presentation of ideal features is somewhat list-like and although the suggestions were connected to previous research, this was not elaborated on. Most likely, the candidate had run out of time and was quickly jotting down as much as possible in the remaining minutes. This is unfortunate as this part of the question

*is worth 10 marks. This illustrates the importance of using your time
well. This section is awarded 4/10 marks, which gives a question total
of 18/34 marks, equivalent to a grade D.*

KEY STUDY

Article 1

**Carol Rowe (1999) 'Do social stories benefit children with autism in
mainstream primary schools?', *British Journal of Special Education*
26 (1), 12–14.**

A case study regarding intervention

Aim

The author was interested in investigating the effect of a social story
on one boy's disruptive lunchtime behaviour.

The study

A social story's approach involves providing an individually designed
narrative for a social situation which the child finds difficult. This
approach was developed in America by Gray (1994) and provides:

- Descriptive information regarding what the situation is and why it
  is happening.
- Perspective information outlining responses and reactions of others.
- Directive information outlining desired and appropriate responses
  for the child.

This approach is seen as useful for children within the autistic spectrum.
George, diagnosed as having Asperger's syndrome, was a Year 2 pupil
in a mainstream school and was the subject of this case study. George
was experiencing difficulties with social interactions, in particular he
was finding lunchtime traumatic. The following observation is typical
of George's behaviour.

> As it was time for lunch, George went with his support assistant
> to collect his lunch box. As George was doing so, he was

complaining very loudly to his support assistant that he did not want to eat with the other children. No amount of reasoning seemed to have any effect. George refused to pick up his lunch box, shouting that the other children were too noisy and were disgusting as they ate with their mouths open. George's support assistant was unable to persuade him to have lunch with the other children.

It was thought that George could benefit from a social story. Teachers, all other relevant adults, and George were interviewed to gauge their view of the problem. For a social story to work, it is paramount that the child's perspectives and feelings be addressed. A social story was written in the form of a three-page booklet, and this was read before lunchtimes.

Lunch Time

- Before Lunch I am usually in the playground.
- A dinner lady tells me when it is time to go and have lunch.
- I get my lunch box and then I walk to the hall.
- When I go into the hall for lunch there are lots of people there. Usually it is not just my class.
- A grown up usually shows me where to sit.
- Children often like to talk while they are eating.
- There are lots of children in the hall who are talking at the same time.
- If the children get too noisy a grown up asks them to talk quietly.
- Sometimes children forget to close their mouths when they are eating.
- I will try to stay calm and quiet if I see children opening their mouths when they are eating.
- I will try to eat my own lunch and not worry about the way the other children are eating their lunch.

(Rowe 1999, p. 13)

Results

When this story was first read to George his immediate reply was that he now knew what he should do. He consequently went with his support assistant and collected his lunch box, went into the hall and ate his lunch. George's behaviour was monitored for twelve weeks. Lunch times had now become happy times for George and after six weeks the frequency with which the story was read was decreased. After twelve weeks George no longer needed to read the story, as 'he remembered it', and it was apparent that this appropriate behaviour had generalised to new situations such as assemblies.

Discussion

In summary, the author feels that social stories are a useful intervention technique. However, as the investigation was an individual case study, the extent to which social stories will work with all individuals with autism, in all situations, needs to be further examined.

Article 2

Robert Rosenthal and Lenore Jacobson (1966) 'Teachers' expectancies: determinants of pupils' IQ gains', *Psychological Reports* 19, 115–118.

Aim

The aim of this study was to determine to what extent teacher expectations influence students' performance on an IQ test.

The study

A test of non–verbal intelligence was administered to all children within an elementary school. The school consisted of six grades, or year groups, with three classes per year group. On average 20 per cent of the children from any one class were chosen to be part of the experimental group. In terms of the study, the experimental group consisted of particular children who were identified to the teachers on the basis of test results. Specifically teachers were told: 'their scores on the test for intellectual blooming indicated that these students would show unusual intellectual gains during the academic year.' In actual fact the students were assigned randomly to the experimental condition. Eight months later all children were re-tested.

Results

The results are illustrated in Table 10.1.

Table 10.1 Mean gains in IQ				
Grade	Experimental	Control	Difference	Probability
1	27	12	15	0.002
2	16.5	7	9.5	0.02
3	5	5	0	
4	5.6	2.2	3.4	
5	17.4	17.5	−0.1	
6	10.0	10.7	−0.7	
Weighted mean	12.22	8.4	3.8	0.02

Discussion

Although the weighted mean suggests an overall effect, it is clear that teachers' expectations operated primarily on the younger children in grades 1 and 2. The authors speculated that a number of factors could be contributing to the results.

- Younger children have less established reputations, so making the predictions more credible in the mind of the teacher.
- Younger children may be more susceptible to teachers' responses created by raised expectations.
- The differences between younger and older children might include other characteristics in addition to age.
- Teachers of lower grades may differ from teachers of higher grades on a number of dimensions that might be related to communicating effectively raised expectations.

When this study was originally published it had a huge impact due to the implications it had for the field of teaching. If positive expectations can increase performance, then perhaps negative expectations, based on factors such as background, reputation or performance in previous tests, can decrease performance.

However, the initial study was criticised on methodological grounds. The IQ test that was used on the younger subjects was not standardised. Attempts at replicating Rosenthal and Jacobson's results have been mixed. Many have failed, while others have upheld the link between expectations and achievement. It is now thought that teachers' expectations influence students' self-esteem which in turn has an effect on student performance.

Glossary

The first occurrence of each of these terms is highlighted in **bold** type in the main text.

accommodation A term used by Piaget to describe the modification of schemas to incorporate new experiences.

adaptation Adaptation according to Piaget encompasses the changes the individual makes in response to the environment. The changes involve the development of schemas through the processes of assimilation and accommodation.

ADHD Attention Deficit Hyperactivity Disorder is cited by the DSM-IV as a condition marked by excessive activity and problems in regard to sustained attention and high levels of impulsivity.

assessment Assessment can be defined as a tool which involves the collection of data for the purpose of decision making.

assimilation A Piagetian term to describe how new information is fitted into existing schemas.

attribution theory In its most general sense, how an individual interprets, perceives or explains the behaviour of themselves or another.

cognition Development of intellectual processes including thinking, understanding, knowing, reasoning and problem solving.

co-morbidity The degree to which one health condition is associated with another condition.

concrete operational stage The third of Piaget's four stages of cognitive development. The stage lasts from approximately the age of 7 or 8 until the age of 11 or 12. The child in this stage has developed mental operations, or rules of logic, for dealing with the world but is limited by their inability to deal with abstract thought.

conditioned response Within classical conditioning, a response elicited by a conditioned stimulus.

conditioned stimulus Within classical conditioning, a stimulus, which initially does not elicit any response but comes to do so by being paired with an unconditioned stimulus.

conserve A Piagetian term to describe the child's awareness that an object will only have changed if something has been added or subtracted. The child realises that volume or quantity does not change even if appearance does.

decentre A Piagetian term to describe the child's ability to hold and understand in their mind multiple and sometimes apparently conflicting aspects of a situation. This ability is first seen in children in the concrete operational stage.

discovery learning An approach which sees active individual effort as being responsible for the acquisition of new knowledge.

Down's syndrome A condition caused by a chromosomal anomaly, where instead of there being 46 chromosomes within each cell, there are 47. This is the result of an extra chromosome 21.

dyslexia Difficulty learning to read and spell despite adequate intelligence, instruction and opportunity.

egocentrism A Piagetian term to describe the tendency of a child to believe that others see things from their perspective.

elementary mental functions A term coined by Vygotsky to denote natural unlearned mental capacities such as attending and sensing.

emotional behavioural difficulties (EBD) Behaviour which challenges the teacher. The behaviour, while not acceptable, is within normal bounds and is not behaviour that can be attributed to any form of mental illness.

enactive representation A term used by Bruner to convey a way of representing the world by internalising physical actions to form a muscle memory.

errorless learning A learning programme in which it is the teacher's responsibility to ensure that the student experiences only successes.

formal operational stage The final stage of cognitive development according to Piaget. This stage, beginning at approximately age 11 or 12, is characterised by the ability to use abstract rules of logic.

general symbolic function One of the key accomplishments of the sensori-motor stage of development, encompassing the emergence of language, deferred imitation and make-believe play.

higher mental functions A term used by Vygotsky to describe learned mental capacities such as thinking and problem solving. These capacities would be learned through social interactions.

iconic mode A term used by Bruner to describe a way of representing the world through concrete images, be they visual, sound or smell.

intersubjectivity Denotes a shared understanding which according to Vygotsky is achieved through dialogue.

learned helplessness A term coined by Seligman which implies a helplessness which is learned through exposure to inescapable unpleasant situations, and then generalised to other situations where escape is possible.

learning style An individual's preference in regard to the context in which information to be learned is presented and how that information is processed.

locus of control An individual's perception in regard to whether their own behaviour is controlled by internal factors or external factors.

mental operations A Piagetian term describing the cognitive ability to apply rules of logic.

meta-cognition An individual's awareness and knowledge concerning their own thinking and problem-solving abilities.

nurture groups A pyschodynamic approach targeting young children who have emotional and behavioural problems. The approach sees the child's difficulties as the result of attachment problems and aims to provide a warm and supportive environment where the child can find value in themselves and develop more appropriate forms of behaviour.

object permanence A Piagetian term describing the realisation that objects continue to exist in time and space regardless of whether an individual can see them or not.

phonemes Distinctive sound units which in combination form words.

Picture Exchange Communication System or PECS A treatment for autism which targets language development. To begin with, a student is required to exchange a picture of a desired object for the object itself. This system utilising pictures goes on to encourage communication through combinations of pictures which correspond to sentences.

pre-operational stage This is the second of Piaget's stages of cognitive development, lasting from approximately 2 to 7 years of age. This stage is characterised by the inability of the child to apply mental operations or rules of logic.

scaffolding A concept used by Vygotsky and expanded upon by Bruner to describe the process by which a more skilled individual teaches a less skilled individual.

schemas Organised patterns or units of action or thought which we construct to make sense of our interactions with the world.

self-efficacy A personal estimate in regard to our own personal effectiveness.

semiotic mediation The process which according to Vygotsky achieves a shared understanding or intersubjectivity.

sensori-motor stage This is the first of Piaget's stages of cognitive development, beginning with birth and lasting until approximately 2 years of age. The key achievements of this stage are the development of object permanence and general symbolic function.

spiral curriculum A term used by Bruner which describes how concepts over time are developed and re-developed with increasing complexity.

statement A legal document issued by a local education authority where it has been found upon investigation that an individual has special educational needs.

symbolic mode A way of representing the world, according to Bruner, which is characterised by the use of arbitrary symbols.

unconditioned response Within classical conditioning, a reflex response that is elicited by an unconditioned stimulus.

unconditioned stimulus Within classical conditioning, a stimulus that has the natural ability to evoke an unconditioned response or reflex reaction.

Yerkes-Dodson Law Refers to the relationship between performance and arousal, with tasks having differing levels of optimal arousal resulting in maximum performance.

Zone of Proximal Development Vygotsky referred to this as the difference between what an individual could achieve by themselves and what they could achieve with assistance. Vygotsky saw this difference as measuring individuals' potential to learn.

Answers to Progress exercises

Chapter 1

1.1 Missing phrases: existing schemas, cognitive equilibrium, assimilation, new experience, dis-equilibrium, accommodate.

    Piaget's theory could not account for this. It would seem that developing new schemas involves more than cognitive dis-equilibrium.

Chapter 2

2.1 UCR = humiliation, CS = thinking of or doing maths, CR = fear of humiliation.

Chapter 6

6.1 Missing phrases: 1 learning styles, 2 cognitive styles, 3 learning strategy, 4 teaching style

6.2 1 = activist, 2 = reflector, 3 = theorist, 4 = pragmatist.

Bibliography

Aaron, P.G., Kuchta, S. and Grapenthin, C.T. (1988) Is there a thing called dyslexia? *Annals of Dyslexia*, 38, 33–49.

Ackerly, B. and Lomas, J. (1998) An environmental audit, in *Approaches to Working with Children with Multiple Disabilities and a Visual Impairment*, London: on behalf of Vital by RNIB.

Aggleton, P. (1987) *Rebels Without a Cause: Middle Class Youth and the Transition from School to Work*, Lewes: Falmer Press.

Ahonen, T., Luotoniemi, A., Nokelainen, K., Savelius, A. and Tasola, S. (1994) Multi-modal intervention in children with attention-deficit hyperactivity disorder, *European Journal of Special Needs Education*, 9(2), 168–179.

Alloway, N. and Gilbert, P. (1997) Boys and literacy: lessons from Australia, *Gender and Education*, 9(1), 49–58.

APA (1995) *Diagnostic and Statistical Manual of Mental Disorders*, 4th edn, Washington.

—— (1996) *A.P.A. Task Force Examines the Knowns and Unknowns of Intelligence*, Online, available HTTP: http://www.apa.org/releases/intell.html (17 April 2000).

Arnot, M., Gray, J., James, M. and Rudduck, J. (1998) *A Review of Recent Research on Gender and Educational Performance*, OFSTED Research Series, London: The Stationery Office.

Arnot, M., David, M. and Weiner, G. (1999) *Closing the Gender Gap: Postwar Education and Social Change*, Cambridge: Polity Press.

Ashman, A. and Conway, R. (1993) *Using Cognitive Methods in the Classroom*, London: Routledge.

Atkinson, R.L., Atkinson, R.C., Smith, E.E. and Bem, D.J. (1993) *Introduction to Psychology*, 11th edn, New York: Harcourt, Brace, Jovanovich.

Atkinson, S. (1999) Circle games, *Primary Maths and Science*, July/August, 17–21.

Bandura, A. (1986) *Social Foundations of Thought and Action: A Social Cognitive Theory*, Englewood Cliffs, NJ: Prentice-Hall.

Bannatyne, A.D. (1971) *Language, Reading and Learning Disabilities*, Springfield, Ill.: Thomas.

Barkley, R.A. (1998) Attention Deficit Hyperactivity Disorder, *Scientific American*, Sept., 44–49.

Bee, H. (1989) *The Developing Child*, 5th edn, New York: Harper-Collins.

—— (1997) *The Developing Child*, 8th edn, New York: Longman.

Bennathan, M. (1997) Effective intervention in primary schools: what nurture groups achieve, *Emotional and Behavioural Difficulties*, 2(3), Winter, 23–29.

Bennett, S.I. (1990) *Comprehensive Multicultural Education, Theory and Practice*, Boston: Allyn & Bacon.

Bleach, K. and Smith, J. (1998) Switching off and dropping out? *Topic*, Autumn, Issue 20, 1–5.

Boaler, J. (1997) *Experiencing School Mathematics: Teaching Styles, Sex and Setting*, Milton Keynes: Open University Press.

Bondy, A.S. and Frost, L.A. (1994) The Picture Exchange Communication System, *Focus on Autistic Behavior*, 9(3), August, 1–19.

Bowers, P. (1987) *The Effect of the 4MAT System on Achievement and Attitudes in Science*, ERIC NO: ED292660.

Bowlby, J. (1965) *Child Care and the Growth of Love*, 2nd edn, Harmondsworth: Penguin Books.

Brehm, S.S. and Kassin, S.M. (1990) *Social Psychology*, Boston: Houghton Mifflin.

Brehm, J.W. and Self, E.A. (1989) The intensity of motivation, *Annual Review of psychology*, 40, 109–131.

Brooks, P. (1995) A comparison of the effectiveness of different teaching strategies in teaching spelling to a student with severe specific learning difficulties/dyslexia, *Educational and Child Psychology*, 12(1), 80–88.

Brown, W.F. and Forristall, D.A. (1983) *Computer-Assisted Study Skills Improvement Program*, ERIC NO: ED234295.

Bruner, J.S. (1963) *The Process of Education*, Cambridge, Mass.: Harvard University Press.

—— (1966) On the conservation of liquids. In J.S. Bruner, R.R. Oliver and P.M. Greenfield (eds) *Studies in Cognitive Growth*, New York: Wiley.

Bryan, B., Dadzie, S. and Scafe, S. (1985) *The Heart of the Race*, London: Virago.

Bryant, P. and Bradley, L. (1985) *Children's Reading Problems*, Oxford: Blackwell.

Bull, S.L. and Solity, J.E. (1987) *Classroom Management: Principles to Practice*, London: Croom Helm.

Centre for the Study of Inclusive Education (1996) *Developing an Inclusive Policy for Your School: A CSIE Guide*, Bristol: CSIE.

Charlton, T. and David, K. (eds) (1993) *Managing Misbehaviour in Schools*, London: Routledge.

Chi, M.T.H. and Glaser, R. (1980) The measurement of expertise: analysis of the development of knowledge and skill as a basis for assessing achievement, in E.L. Baker and E.S. Quellmalz (eds) *Educational Testing and Evaluation: Design, Analysis and Policy*, Beverly Hills, Calif.: Sage.

Chisholm, L. and du Bois-Reymond, M. (1993) Youth transitions, gender and social change, *Sociology*, 27(2), 259–279.

Clarke, S. (1998) *Targeting Assessment in the Primary Classroom*, Abingdon: Hodder & Stoughton.

Cohen, D. (1990) *Essential Psychology*, London: Bloomsbury.

Coleman, J.S. (1961) *The Adolescent Society. The Social Life of the Teenager and its Impact on Education*, Glencoe, Ill.: Free Press.

Cooley, C.H. (1902) *Human Nature and the Social Order*, New York: Scribner.

Cooper, H. and Good, T. (1983) *Pygmalion Grows Up: Studies in the Expectation Communication Process*, New York: Longman.

Cooper, P. (1996) Editorial, *Emotional and Behavioural Difficulties*, 1(1), 1.

Cooper, P. and Lovey, J. (1999) Early intervention in emotional and behavioural difficulties: the role of Nurture Groups, *European Journal of Special Needs Education*, 14(2), 122–131.

Coopersmith, S. (1967) *The Antecedents of Self-esteem*, San Francisco: Freeman.

Corsini, R.J. and Auerbach, A.J. (eds) (1996) *Concise Encyclopaedia of Psychology*, 2nd edn, New York: Wiley.

Cowdery, L., Morse, P., Prince, M. and Montgomery, D. (1983, 1984 and 1985) *Teaching Reading Through Spelling*, Kingston: Kingston Polytechnic Learning Difficulties Project.

Cowne, E. (1996) *The Senco Handbook: Working within a Whole School Approach*, London: David Fulton.

Cox, R. (1991) Motivation, in S.J. Bull (1993) *Sport Psychology: A Self-Help Guide*, Ramsbury: Crowood Press.

Critchley, M. (1970) *The Dyslexic Child*, Springfield, Ill.: Thomas.

Cullingford, C. (1991) *The Inner World of the School: Children's Ideas about Schools*, London: Cassell.

Cumming, J.J. and Maxwell, G.S. (1999) Contextualising authentic assessment, *Assessment in Education*, 6(2), 177–194.

Curry, L. (1983) An organization of learning styles theory and constructs, *ERIC Document*, 235, 185.

Daniels, H., Hey, V., Leonard, D. and Smith, M. (1996) *Gender and Special Needs Provision in Mainstream Schooling*, ESRC End of Award Report, R000235059.

Daniels, H., Visser, J., Cole, T. and Reybekill, N. de (1999) *Emotional and Behavioural Difficulties in Mainstream Schools*, School of Education, University of Birmingham, DfEE, RR90.

Department for Education (1992) *Designing for Pupils with Special Educational Needs, Special Schools*, London: HMSO.

Department for Education (1994a) *The Education of Children with Emotional and Behavioural Difficulties* (Circular 9/94), London: DfEE.

Department for Education (1994b) *Code of Practice on the Identification and Assessment of Special Educational Needs*, London: DfEE.

Department for Education (1995) *The National Curriculum*, London: DfEE.

Department for Education and Employment (1997a) *Excellence for All Children: Meeting Special Education Needs* (Green Paper), London: The Stationery Office.

Department for Education and Employment (1997b) *Excellence in Schools* (White Paper), London: The Stationery Office.

Department for Education and Employment (1999) *Every school should have a clear policy for gifted children*, Online, available HTTP: http://195.44.11.137/coi/coipress.nsf (2 April 2000).

Department for Education and Employment (2000a) *National Literacy and Numeracy Strategies: Guidance on Teaching Able Children*, London: DfEE.

Department for Education and Employment (2000b) *Removing the Barriers: Raising Achievement Levels for Minority Ethnic Pupils*, London: DfEE.

Department of Education (1981) *The Education Act 1981*.

Department of Education and Science (1989) *Discipline in Schools* (The Elton Report), London: HMSO.

Detweiler, R.E., Hicks, A.P. and Hicks, M.R. (1995) The multi-modal diagnosis and treatment of Attention Deficit Hyperactivity Disorder, *Therapeutic Care and Education*, 4(2), Summer, 4–9.

Devlin, A. (1996) Criminal classes – are there links between failure at school and future offending? *Support for Learning*, 11(1), 13–16.

Donaldson, M. (1978) *Children's Minds*, London: Fontana.

Doran, C. and Cameron, R.J. (1995) Learning about learning: metacognitive approaches in the classroom, *Educational Psychology in Practice*, 11(2), 15–23.

Downing, J.E. (1996) *Including Students with Severe and Multiple Disabilities in Typical Classrooms*, Baltimore, Md: Paul H. Brookes Publishing Co.

Drew, D. and Grey, J. (1990) The fifth year examination achievements of black young people in *England and Wales*, Educational Research, 32(3), 107–117.

Dunn, R. and Dunn, K. (1992) *Teaching Elementary Students through their Individual Learning Styles: Practical Approaches for Grades 3–6*, Boston, Mass.: Allyn & Bacon.

—— (1993) *Teaching Secondary Students through their Individual Learning Styles: Practical Approaches for Grades 7–12*, Boston, Mass.: Allyn & Bacon.

Dunn, R., Dunn, K. and Price, G. (1985) *Manual: Learning Style Inventory*, Lawrence, Kan.: Price Systems.

Dunn, R., Griggs, S. and Price, G. (1993) Learning styles of Mexican-American and Anglo-American elementary-school students, *Journal of Multicultural Counselling and Development*, 21(4), 237–247, EJ470183.

Dweck, C.S. (1975) The role of expectations and attributions in the alleviation of learned helplessness, *Journal of Personality and Social Psychology*, 31, 674–685.

——(1978) Achievement, in M.E. Lamb (ed.) *Social and Personality Development*, New York: Holt, Rinehart & Winston.

Dweck, C.S. and Leggett, E.L. (1988) A social-cognitive approach to motivation and personality, *Psychological Review*, 95, 256–273.

Dyslexia in the Primary Classroom (1997) in *Teaching Today Series*, London: BBC Education in association with British Dyslexia Association.

Dyson, A. (1996) *Managing SEN Policy in Cleveland Primary and Secondary Schools*, Online, available HTTP: wwwmailbase.ac.uk/lists/senco-forum/files/dysonma96 html (3 January 2000).

Edelson, S.M. (2000) *Learning Styles and Autism*, Centre for Study of Autism, Salem, Oreg. Online, available HTTP: http://www.autism.org/styles.html (17 April 2000).

Edwards, C. (1997) Today's lesson: noise in the classroom, *Vibes*, July.

Ellis, A.W. (1993) *Reading, Writing and Dyslexia: A Cognitive Analysis*, 2nd edn, Hove: Erlbaum.

Evans, G.W. and Maxwell, L. (1997) Chronic noise exposure and reading deficits: the mediating effects of language acquisition, *Environment and Behaviour*, 29(5), 638–656.

Faherty, C. (1999) *Structuring for Success*, Online, available HTTP: http://www.unc.edu/depts/teacch/teacch e.htm (3 January 2000).

FEDA (1995) *Learning Styles*, London: Meridan House.

Felder, R.M. (1996) Matter of Style, *ASEE Prism*, 6(4), 18–23.

Fernald, G.M. (1943) *Remedial Techniques in Basic School Subjects*, New York: McGraw-Hill.

Feuerstein, R., Rand, Y., Hoffman, F. and Miller, R. (1980) *Instrumental Enrichment*, Baltimore, Md.: Baltimore University Press.

Field, T.M. (1988) Pre-school play: effects of teacher/child ratios and organisation of the classroom space, *Child Study Journal*, 10(3), 191–205.

Fontana, D. (1995) *Psychology for Teachers*, 3rd edn, London: Macmillan.

Frey, K.S. and Ruble, D.N. (1985) What children say when the teacher is not around: conflicting goals in social comparison and performance assessment in the classroom, *Journal of Personality and Social Psychology*, 48, 550–562.

Galton, M. and Williamson, J. (1992) *Group-Work in the Primary Classroom*, London: Routledge.

Garner, P. and Gains, C. (1996) Models of intervention for children with emotional and behavioural difficulties, *Support for Learning*, 11(4), 141–145.

Garner P. and Hill, N. (1995) *What Teachers Do: Developments in Special Education*, London: Paul Chapman.

Gavienas, E. (1999) *The Dilemma: Seating Arrangements for Group Teaching*, The Scottish Council for Research in Education, Online, available HTTP: http://www.scre.ac.uk/nl61gavienas.html (17 April 2000).

Gerald, M. (1998) Uses and abuses of the multi-sensory room, in *Approaches to Working with Children with Multiple Disabilities and a Visual Impairment*, London: on behalf of Vital by RNIB.

Getzels, J. (1974) Images of the classroom and visions of the learner, *School Review*, 82, 527–540.

Gillborn, D. and Gipps, C. (1996) *Recent Research on the Achievements of Ethnic Minority Pupils*, OFSTED Review of Research, London: HMSO.

Gleeson, D. (1994) Wagging, bobbing and bunking-off, *Educational Review*, 46(1), 15–19.

Goleman, D. (1996) *Emotional Intelligence*, London: Bloomsbury.

Grandin, T. (1998) *Teaching Tips for Children and Adults with Autism*, Online, available HTTP: http://www.autism.org/temple/tips.html (18 April, 2000).

Gray, C. (1994) *The Social Story Book*, Arlington: Future Horizons.

Greenhalgh, P. (1994) *Emotional Growth and Learning*, London: Routledge.

Griggs, S. and Dunn, R. (1996) *Hispanic-American Students and Learning Style*, ERIC Digest.

Griggs, S.A. (1991) *Learning Styles Counselling*, ERIC Digest.

Hardwick, J. (1996) Irregular little beasties, *Special Children*, June/July, 7–10.

—— (1997) The hidden alphabet, *Special Children*, March, 13–15.

Harré, R. (1979) *Social Being*, Oxford: Blackwell.

Harter, S. (1981) A new self-report scale of intrinsic vs. extrinsic orientation in the classroom: motivational and informational components, *Developmental Psychology*, 17, 300–312.

—— (1982) The perceived competence scale for children, *Child Development*, 53, 87–97.

Hayes, N. (1994) *Foundations of Psychology*, London: Routledge.

Head, G. and O'Neill, W. (1999) Introducing Feuerstein's Instrumental Enrichment in a school for children with social, emotional and behavioural difficulties, *Support for Learning*, 14(3), 122–128.

Hegarty, S. (1987) *Meeting Special Needs in Ordinary Schools*, London: Cassell.

Honey, P. and Mumford, A. (1986) *Using your Learning Styles*, Maidenhead: Peter Honey.

—— (1992) *The Manual of Learning Styles*, Maidenhead: Peter Honey.

Howlin, P. (1997) *Autism: Preparing for Adulthood*, London: Routledge.

Howlin, P. and Yates, P. (1996) *Increasing social communication skills in young adults with autism attending a social group* (submitted for publication) (as cited in Howlin 1997).

Hudgens, B. (1993) The relationship of cognitive style, planning ability and locus of control to achievement for three ethnic groups (Anglo, African-American, Hispanic), *Dissertation Abstracts International*, A53-08, 2744.

Hughes, M. (1975) *Egocentrism in pre-school children*, Edinburgh University: unpublished doctoral dissertation.

Hull, C. (1943) *Principles of Behaviour Theory*, New York: Appleton, Century, Crofts.

Iszatt, J. and Wasilewska, T. (1997) Nurture Groups: an early intervention model enabling vulnerable children with emotional and behavioural difficulties to integrate successfully into school, *Educational and Child Psychology*, 14(3), 121–139.

Jamieson, J.J. (1994) Teaching as transaction: Vygotskian perspectives on deafness and mother–child interaction, *Exceptional Children*, 60(5), 434–449.

Johnson, D.W. and Johnson, R.T. (1994) *Learning Together and Alone: Co-operative, Competitive and Individualistic Learning*, 4th edn, Boston, Mass.: Allyn & Bacon.

Johnson, D.W., Johnson, R.T., Holubec, E. and Roy, P. (1984) *Circles of Learning: Co-operation in the Classroom*. Alexandria, Va.: Association for Supervision and Curriculum Development.

Johnson, F. and Jamison, J. (1998) *The Impact of Class Size: An Interim Research Summary*, Nfer, Online, available HTTP: http://www.nfer.ac.uk/summary/clasize.htm (20 April 2000).

Johnson, M.K., Springer, S.P. and Sternglanz, S.H. (1982) *How to Succeed in College*, Los Altos, Calif.: William Kaufman.

Keating, D.P. (1980) Thinking processes in adolescence, in J. Adelson (ed.) *Handbook of Adolescent Psychology*, New York: Wiley, pp. 211–246.

Keys, W. (1997) England's performance in the Third International Mathematics and Science Study (TIMSS): implications for educators and policy makers, *Topic 19*, Bonus Item 1, 1–7.

Kirschenbaum, H. (1975) What is humanistic education? in T.B. Roberts (ed.) *Four Psychologies Applied to Education*, New York: Wiley.

Kirschenbaum, H. and Land Henderson, V. (eds) (1990) *The Carl Rogers Reader*, London: Constable.

Kolb, D.A. (1976) *The Learning Styles Inventory: Technical Manual*, Boston, Mass.: McBer & Company.

—— (1977) *Learning Styles Inventory: A Self Description of Preferred Learning Modes*, Boston, Mass.: McBer & Company.

—— (1984) *Experiential Learning: Experience as the Source of Learning and Development*, Englewood Cliffs, NJ: Prentice-Hall.

Kyriacou, D. (1991) *Essential Teaching Skills*, Oxford: Blackwell.

LaHoste, G.J., Swanson, J.M., Wigal, S.B., Glabe, D., Wigal, T., King, N. and Kennedy, J.L. (1996) Dopamine D4 receptor gene polymorphism is associated with Attention Deficit Hyperactivity Disorder, *Molecular Psychiatry*, 1(2), 122–124.

LeFrancois, G.R. (1997) *Psychology for Teaching*, 9th edn, Belmont, Calif.: Wadsworth.

Leland-Jones, P.J. (1997) *Improving the Acquisition of Sixth-Grade Social Studies Concepts through the Implementation of a Study Skills Unit*, ERIC NO: ED424154.

Lewis, A. (1995) *Children's Understanding of Disability*, London: Routledge.

Lewis, B.N. (1976) Avoidance of aptitude-treatment trivialities, in S. Messick (ed.) *Individuality in Learning*, San Francisco, Calif.: Jossey-Bass.

Mac an Ghaill, M. (1994) *The Making of Men: Masculinities, Sexualities and Schooling*, Buckingham: Open University Press.

McCarthy, B. (1990) *Using the 4 MAT System to Bring Learning Styles to Schools*, ERIC NO: EJ416429.

McClelland, D.C. (1985) How motives, skills and values determine what people do, *American Psychologist*, 40, 812–825.

McClelland, D.C., Atkinson, J.W., Clark, R.A. and Lowell, E.L. (1953) *The Achievement Motive*, New York: Appleton-Century-Crofts.

McGarrigle, J. and Donaldson, M. (1974) Conservation accidents, *Cognition*, 3, 341–50.

McGuiness, J. and Craggs, D. (1986) Disruption as a school-generated problem, in D.P. Tattum (ed.) *Management of Disruptive Behaviour in Schools*, Chichester: Wiley.

Maslow, A.H. (1954) *Motivation and Personality* (2nd edn, 1970), New York: Harper & Row.

Maxwell, L. and Evans, G.W. (2000) *Design of Child Care Centers and Effects of Noise on Young Children*, Online, available HTTP: http:/www.designshare.com/Research/LMaxwell/NoiseChildren.htm (20 April 2000).

Mead, G.H. (1934) *Mind, Self and Society*, Chicago, Ill.: University of Chicago Press.

Mercer, N. (1995) *The Guided Construction of Knowledge*, Clevedon: Multilingual Matters Ltd.

Miles, T.R. and Miles, E. (1990) *Dyslexia: A Hundred Years On*, Milton Keynes: Open University Press.

Miller-Jones, D. (1989) Culture and testing, *American Psychologist*, 44, 343–348.

Mirza, H.S. (1997) Black women in education: a collective movement, in H.S. Mirza (ed.) *Black British Feminism: A Reader*, London: Routledge.

Modood, T. and Shiner, M. (1994) *Ethnic Minorities and Higher Education: Why are there Differential Rates of Entry?* London: Policy Studies Institute.

Molnar, A. and Lindquist, G. (1989) *Changing Problem Behaviour in Schools*: San Francisco, Calif.: Jossey-Bass.

Moyles, J.R. (1992) *Organizing for Learning in the Primary Classroom*, Buckingham: Open University Press.

Myers, I.B. (1962) *The Myers-Briggs Type Indicator Manual*, Princeton, NJ: Educational Testing Service.

Nash, B.C. (1981) The effects of classroom spatial organisation on four and five year old children learning, *British Journal of Educational Psychology*, 51, 44–55.

National Association for Gifted Children (2000) *Developing a School Policy for Gifted and Very Able Children*, Online, available HTTP: http://www.rmplc.co.uk/orgs/nagc/index.html (2 April 2000).

Neill, S.R. St J. (1991) *Classroom Non-Verbal Communication*, London: Routledge.

Neisser, U. (1997) Rising scores on intelligence tests, *American Scientist*, Online, available HTTP: http://i/articles/97articles/neisser.html (19 May 2001).

Newmann, F.M. and Archbald, D.A. (1992) The nature of authentic academic achievement, in H. Berlak, F.M. Newmann, E. Adams, D.A. Archbald, T. Burgess, J. Raven and T.A. Romberg, *Towards a New Science of Educational Testing and Assessment*, Albany, NY: State University of New York Press.

Newton, M.J. and Thompson, M.E. (1976) *The Aston Index: A Screening Procedure for Written Language Difficulties*, Wisbech: Learning Developmental Aids.

Nfer-Nelson (2000) *Cognitive Ability Test*, Online, available HTTP: http://www.nfer-nelson.co.uk/cat/index.htm (2 October 2000).

Nfer Press Release (1998) 'Counting the cost of reducing class size', 18 September 1998, Online, available HTTP: http://www.nfer.ac.uk/press/class.htm (2 April 2000).

Noble, C. (1999) Raising boys' achievement, *Topic*, Issue 22, 1–4.

Ockelford, A. (1998) Making sense of the world, in *Approaches to Working with Children with Multiple Disabilities and a Visual Impairment*, London: on behalf of Vital by RNIB.

OFSTED/EOC (1996) *The Gender Divide: Performance Differences Between Boys and Girls at School*, London: HMSO.

Ogilvy, C.M. (1994) An evaluation review of approaches to behaviour problems in the secondary school, *Educational Psychology*, 14(2), 195–206.

ONS (2000) *Social Trends 2000*, London: The Stationery Office.

Papalia, D.F. (1972) The status of several conservative abilities across the life-span, *Human Development*, 15, 229–243.

Parsons, C. (1996) Permanent exclusions from schools in England in the 1990s: trends, causes and responses, *Children and Society*, 10, 177–186.

Piaget, J. (1954) *The Construction of Reality in the Child*, New York: Basic Books.

—— (1970a) *The Science of Education and the Psychology of the Child*, New York: Viking Press.

—— (1970b) Piaget's theory, in P.H. Mussen (ed.) *Carmichael's Manual of Child Psychology*, New York: Wiley.

—— (1971) *Structuralism*, London: Routledge & Kegan Paul.

Pickard, J. (1998) Dynamic testing reveals real abilities of drop-outs, *People Management*, 28, May, 11.

Preston, M. (1998) Including children with Autistic Spectrum disorder, *Special Children*, Nov./Dec., 15–17.

Putnam, J. (ed.) (1993) *Co-operative Learning and Strategies for Inclusion: Celebrating Diversity in the Classroom*, Baltimore, Md.: Paul H. Brookes Publishing Co.

Ramjhun, A.F. (1995) *Implementing the Code of Practice for Children with Special Educational Needs*, London: David Fulton.

Reber, A.S. (1985) *The Penguin Dictionary of Psychology*, Aylesbury: Penguin Books

Reiff, J.C. (1992) *Learning Styles*, Washington, DC: National Education Association.

Renshaw, P. (1990) Self-esteem research and equity programs, in J. Kenway and S. Willis (eds) *Hearts and Minds*, Lewes: Falmer Press.

Reybekill, N. de (1998) *Alternative or free: alternatives to Mainstream education for disaffected adolescents in Denmark*, unpublished doctoral dissertation, University of Birmingham, Birmingham.

Rezler, A.G. and Rezmovic, V. (1981) The learning preference inventory, *Journal of Applied Health*, 10, 28–34.

Richelle, M.N. (1993) *B.F. Skinner: A Reappraisal*, Hove: Erlbaum.

Riding, R. and Cheema, I. (1991) Cognitive styles – an overview and integration, *Educational Psychology*, 11(3 and 4), 193–215.

Robinson, F.P. (1970) *Effective Study*, 4th edn, New York: Harper & Row.

Robinson, H.B. (1981) The uncommonly bright child, in M. Lewis and L.A. Rosenblum (eds) *The Uncommon Child*, New York: Plenum.

Rogers, C. (1957) Personal thoughts on teaching and learning, *Merrill-Palmer Quarterly*, 3, Summer.

—— (1961) *On Becoming a Person: A Therapist's View of Psychotherapy*, London: Constable.

—— (1977) The politics of education, *Journal of Humanistic Education*, 1(1), 6–22.

Rose, R., Fletcher, W. and Goodwin, G. (1999) Pupils with severe learning difficulties as personal target setters, *British Journal of Special Education*, 26(4), 206–212.

Rose, S.A. and Blank, M. (1974) The potency of context in children's cognition: an illustration through conservation, *Child Development*, 45, 499–502.

Rosenthal, R. (1985) From unconscious experimenter bias to teacher expectancy effects, in J.B. Dusek, V.D. Hall and W.J. Meyer (eds) *Teacher Expectancies*, Hillsdale, NJ: Erlbaum.

Rosenthal R. and Jacobson, L. (1966) Teachers' expectancies: determinants of pupils' IQ gains, *Psychological Reports*, 19, 115–118.

—— (1968) *Pygmalion in the Classroom*, New York: Holt, Rinehart & Winston.

Rotter, J.B. (1966) Generalised expectancies for internal vs. external control of reinforcement, *Psychological Monographs*, 80: no. 1.

Rowe, C. (1999) Do social stories benefit children with autism in mainstream primary schools? *British Journal of Special Education*, 26(1), 12–14.

Rubin, K.H., Attewell, P.W., Tierney, M.C. and Tumolo, P. (1973) Development of spatial egocentrism and conservation across the life-span, *Developmental Psychology*, 9, 432–437.

Ruble, D.B. (1983) The development of comparison processes and their role in achievement-related self-socialization, in E.T. Higgins, D.N. Ruble and W.W. Hartup (eds) *Social Cognition and Social Development: A Sociocultural Perspective*, New York: Cambridge University Press.

Salvia, J. and Ysseldyke, J.E. (1998) *Assessment*, Boston, Mass.: Houghton Mifflin.

Sangster, S. and Shulman, R. (1988) *The Impact of the 4 MAT System as a Curriculum Delivery Model*, Research Report, ERIC NO: ED316567.

SED (Scottish Education Department) (1977) *Truancy and Indiscipline in Schools*, Report of the Committee of Enquiry (The Pack Report), Edinburgh: HMSO.

Seligman, M.E.P. (1975) *Helplessness: On Depression, Development and Death*, San Francisco, Calif.: W.H. Freeman.

Seligman, M.E.P. and Maier, S.F. (1967) Failure to escape traumatic shock, *Journal of Experimental Psychology*, 74, 1–9.

Sharp, C., Osgood, J. and Flanagan, N. (1999) *The Benefits of Study Support, a Review of Opinion and Research* (DfEE Research Report 110), Sheffield: DfEE.

Sharron, H. and Coulter, M. (1994) *Changing Children's Minds: Feuerstein's Revolution in the Teaching of Intelligence*, 3rd edn, Birmingham: Sharron Publishing Company.

Shaw, P. (1998) Multi sensory rooms, in *Approaches to Working with Children with Multiple Disabilities and a Visual Impairment*, London: on behalf of Vital by RNIB.

Shaywitz, S.E. (1996) Dyslexia, *Scientific American*, November, 78–84.

Shotter, D. (1997) Smoothing the way, *Special Children*, June/July, 22–25.

Sigelman, C.K. and Shaffer, D.F. (1991) *Life-Span Human Development*, Belmont, Calif.: Brooks/Cole.

Sims, J. (1988) *Learning styles of black-American, Mexican-American, and white American third and fourth grade students in traditional public schools*, doctoral dissertation, University of Santa Barbara, Santa Barbara, Calif.

Skirtic, T. (1991) *Behind Special Education: A Critical Analysis of Professional Culture and School Organisation*, Denver, Colo.: Love Publishing.

Slater, L. (1996) *Welcome to my Country*, London: Hamish Hamilton.

Snow, R.E. and Swanson, J. (1992) Instructional psychology: aptitude, adaptation, and assessment, *Annual Review of Psychology*, 43, 583–626.

The Standards Site (2000) Gender and achievement, DfEE, Online, available HTTP: http://www.standards.dfee.gov.uk/genderandachievement/data_1.1html (5 October 2000).

Sukhnandan, L. (1999) Sorting, sifting and setting, *Nfer News*, Spring.

Sukhnandan, L. and Lee, B. (1998) *Streaming, Setting and Grouping by Ability, a Review of the Literature*, Slough: Nfer.

Swisher, K. (1994) American Indian learning styles survey: an assessment of teachers' knowledge, *The Journal of Educational Issues of Language Minority Students*, 13, 59–77.

Taylor, G. and Thornton, C. (1995) *Managing People*, London: Directory of Social Change.

Thomson, M. (1990) *Developmental Dyslexia*, 3rd edn, London: Whurr Publishers.

Thorndike, R.L., Hagen, E. and France, N. (1986) *Cognitive Ability Test*, 2nd edn, Windsor: Nfer-Nelson.

Tomlinson, S. (1982) *The Sociology of Special Education*, London: Routledge & Kegan Paul.

Tyrer, P. and Steinberg, G.D. (1993) *Models for Mental Disorder*, 2nd edn, Chichester: Wiley.

Vellutino, F.R. (1979) *Dyslexia – Theory and Research*, Cambridge, Mass.: MIT Press.

Violand Hainer, E., Fagan, B., Bratt, T., Baker, L. and Arnold, N. (1990) Integrating learning styles and skills in the ESL classroom: an approach to lesson planning, *NCBE Program Information Guide Series*, No. 2, Summer, Online, available HTTP: http://www.ncbe.gwu.edu/ncbepubs/pigs/pig2.htm (4 April 2000).

Wechsler, D. (1974) *Manual for the Wechsler Intelligence Scale for Children – Revised*, Cleveland, Ohio: Psychological Corporation.

Weiner, B. (1974) *Achievement and Attribution Theory*, Morristown, NJ: General Learning Press.

—— (1986) *An Attribution Theory of Motivation and Emotion*, New York: Springer-Verlag.

Weiten, W. (1989) *Psychology: Themes and Variations*, Pacific Grove, Calif.: Brooks/Cole.

Wertsch, J.V. (1984) The Zone of Proximal Development: some conceptual issues, in B. Rogoff and J.V. Wertsch (eds) *Children's Learning in the 'Zone of Proximal Development'*, San Francisco, Calif.: Jossey-Bass.

—— (1985) *Vygotsky and the Social Formation of Mind*, Cambridge, Mass.: Harvard University Press.

Whalen, C.K. and Henker, B. (1991) Therapies for hyperactive children: comparisons, combinations and compromises, *Journal of Consulting and Clinical Psychology*, 59, 126–137.

White, J. (1986) The writing on the wall: beginning or end of a girl's career? *Women's Studies International Forum*, 9(5), 561–574.

White, R.W. (1959) Motivation reconsidered: the concept of competence, *Psychological Review*, 66, 297–333.

Wiggins, G.P. (1993) *Assessing Student Performance*, San Francisco, Calif.: Jossey-Bass.

Wilkinson, C. (1988) Arranging the classroom environment, in I. Craig (ed.) *Managing the Primary Classroom*, Harlow: Longman.

Wood, D., Bruner, J.S. and Ross, G. (1976) The role of tutoring in problem solving, *Journal of Child Psychology and Psychiatry*, 17, 89–100.

Wood, D.J. (1998) *How Children Think and Learn*, 2nd edn, Oxford: Blackwell.

Wragg, T. (1997) *Assessment and Learning*, London: Routledge.

Yong, F. and Ewing, N. (1992) A comparative study of the learning style preferences among gifted African-American, Mexican-American and American born Chinese middle-grade students, *Roeper Review*, 14(3), 120–123.

Zimmerman, B.J., Bandura, A. and Martinez-Pons, M. (1992) Self-motivation for academic attainment: the role of self-efficacy beliefs and personal goal setting, *American Educational Research Journal*, 29, 663–676.

Index